They Even Took My Shoes

How a journalist overcame betrayal, an
abusive court system, and kept her promise

Paula Fidalgo

Dedication

I am deeply grateful to dedicate this book to my three children, Jerry, Nicole, and Isabella. Little did I know that they would be my greatest source of inspiration, propelling me from a place of adversity to one of resilience and survival. They are the unsung heroes of my world, alongside the Divine guidance of God. I am immensely proud of each of them.

Furthermore, I extend this dedication to my remarkable parents, John and Odilia Fidalgo, whose unwavering support and exemplary values taught me the essence of family, hard work, persistence, and, above all, faith in God. Though my father departed on February 6, 2020, his presence continues to guide me. I shared a part of this book with him in his final days, witnessing his joy before his passing. His kindness lives on within me, a legacy I cherish. I am equally indebted to my resilient mother, whose strength and perseverance have been a beacon of hope in my life's journey.

Testimonials

Paula Fidalgo's book, *They Even Took My Shoes*, is extremely important as she exposes the legal and financial abuse that can happen to anyone, especially in New York State, where there is no judicial oversight, transparency, and accountability. Paula is an overcomer who is taking a stand against egregious injustices that can happen to anyone.

~**Mary Petri**, Slam the Gavel podcast and author of *Dismantling Family Court Corruption, Cry Out for Justice, Poems of Truth,* and *Raised by These Wolves: How Family and Federal Courts Are Failing Our Children*

I am honored to endorse Paula's book, *They Even Took My Shoes*, and celebrate Maria's courageous journey. Maria bravely reveals the trials and tribulations she endured and guides the reader through her journey of resilience. Maria's story is a powerful reminder of the transformative potential inherent within each of us. This book will serve as a beacon of hope and empowerment for anyone navigating hardship. It will teach them to apply the principles of Positive Psychology for a life of freedom and wellbeing.

~**Emiliya Zhivotovskaya,** CEO at The Flourishing Center, NY, NY

I was engrossed by Paula Fidalgo's words from the first sentence. She vividly and eloquently describes her main character Maria Crowe's turbulent journey through her ex-husband's vengeful accusation that ends up destroying her career. She takes us on a journey that illustrates her deep faith in God and her intense love for her three children as she finds herself embroiled in courtroom drama. The reader will feel buoyed by Maria's courage, her ability to forgive, and her blossoming belief in herself. This book will surely inspire anyone going through a hard time to stay the course and focus on the light at the end of the tunnel. As Fidalgo writes, "In the face of such injustice, I resolve to uncover the lessons buried within this trial determined to emerge stronger, wiser, and more resilient than before." A story full of hope.

~**Shelley Lippman**, Author of *As Is: Accepting, Forgiving and Empowering Your Child with ADHD...and Yourself.*

Just hearing the word "divorce" invokes a bit of PTSD in almost everyone. Knowing someone you love has turned into a stranger is heartbreaking. But in the case of Fidalgo's main character, Maria Crowe, knowing that same person is also trying to destroy you is something few can comprehend.

This book reflects the true grit of women such as Maria Crowe, who have dealt with extreme adversity and not only survived but came out stronger, sharing what they learned with all who are open and willing to live with more positivity.

~**Steven Conklin**, Owner of Extreme Bucket List, Public Speaker at Adventure Speakers Bureau, Olympic Bobsled Coach, Australian Bobsled Freelance

Acknowledgments

A heartfelt thank you to my cousins Danny, Diane, Nelson, Tanya, and Johnny, who stood by me during the darkest times when no one else was there for me. Their unwavering support served as a constant reminder of the power of family bonds.

To Greg Rinckey, a big thank you. Your words provided the final push I needed to bring this book to publication. Sometimes, a simple word of encouragement can instill the confidence we need to pursue our dreams, and you did that for me without even realizing it. I'm immensely grateful for the safe space, which allowed me to gather the courage to see this project through to the end. I love you with all my heart.

In a world where angels often go unrecognized, I've been blessed with the presence of Nancy Acemoglu in my life. She's more than a friend; she's been a pillar of strength, a guiding light, a big sister, and a second mother to both me and my children. Through every trial and triumph, she stood by me and my family, offering support and selfless assistance without ever seeking anything in return. Her friendship is a treasure I'll forever hold dear, filled with shared laughter and tears and a testament to the profound impact one person can have on another's life.

In addition to Nancy's support, I must also express my deepest gratitude to my friend Brian Lyda. Brian's belief in me and his encouragement provided the confidence and boost I needed to embrace my new life and career path. He empowered me to take ownership of my entrepreneurship journey, offering guidance and inspiration every step of the way. His mentorship has been invaluable, and I am forever thankful for his belief in my potential.

To my cherished friend Janet O'Boyle, I am profoundly grateful for your dedication to guiding me on my spiritual journey. Your boundless generosity, steadfast support, and tireless efforts have illuminated my path, instilling within me a deep understanding of faith, God, and the teachings of Jesus. Your selflessness and unconditional love never falter, even in the face of adversity. Thank you for sharing your wisdom, time, and heart with me, enriching my life in ways I can never fully express. You have truly been a blessing, and I am forever grateful for your presence in my life.

I extend my deepest gratitude to a dear friend who will remain anonymous, who stood by my side during one of the most profound traumas of my life. I'll forever be grateful.

Rosemarie Clemovich, my confidant and dear friend. Her constant presence throughout the highs and lows of my journey has been an invaluable source of strength and support, from moments of laughter to those of tears and pain; she stood by me as a steadfast companion throughout it all. Thank you for your friendship and for always listening to me without judgment.

Profound thanks to my former student turned friend, Rosa Vidal. Despite the challenges she faced, including caring for her son with a disability, Rosa generously offered her assistance with my children and pets. Her selflessness and boundless compassion speak volumes of her character. Despite her own responsibilities, Rosa dedicated her heart, time, and love to support me and my family. Her kindness knows no bounds, and I am forever grateful for her presence in our lives.

To all my clients from The Dust Busters, whose belief in me paved the path to where I stand today. Your trust and support, especially during times of uncertainty, have been priceless. Your confidence in me has not only propelled me towards financial stability, enabling me to provide for my children, but it has also empowered me to find my voice and emerge stronger than ever before.

I am deeply grateful to Sherry Cavallaro and her son Shay for their exceptional guidance as my real estate agent. Their care, attentiveness, and commitment to understanding my needs resulted in finding the perfect home for my children. Their assistance with unpacking during a challenging time while I was away attending my father's funeral in Portugal was truly invaluable.

Manny Santos, thank you for being a big brother. Your patience, guidance, and authentic advice were invaluable throughout the process. You've been a mentor and a source of wisdom during my comeback journey.

Dan Tuczinski, your friendship and support mean the world to me. Thank you for your kindness.

Michelle Young from Homestead Funding. Thank you for working tirelessly and being dedicated to helping me secure the mortgage to buy my home for my children. You made the impossible possible.

To my former boss at Look TV, Jesse Jackson, thank you for your guidance and encouragement to always maintain integrity, even during challenging times. I'll always remember his advice the day my world came crumbling down and I hit rock bottom, standing in his office, bawling my eyes out, and his advice to rise above, to remain professional, and to stand tall despite what was happening to me. His words serve as a constant reminder to uphold my values and never compromise my principles. Jesse's wisdom continues to guide me, serving as a benchmark for all my actions and decisions.

Peasantman Triathlon Organizers: A big thank you for believing in my talent and honoring me as the queen of your triathlon. Special thanks to Steve, Chris, and Joe for your support and encouragement. Even after my world fell apart and everyone dropped me, you all stood by me. Special shout out to Chris Greklek, who passed away on July 30, 2024, during the final stages of this book and who never got to read this. Thank you. I want his son Taylor and his two daughters, Alexis and Abigail, to know their dad's kindness made a difference in my life, and for that, I will always cherish his soul.

Christina Beauchemin, my Editor, author of *Let My Legacy Be Love*, and founder of Get R.E.A.L. She dedicated her time to help enrich the story by infusing it with painful emotions that were too difficult for me to write. She kept me going when I got stuck towards the end of this publishing process.

A big thank you to Andrea Cowell, from the Mechanicville Domestic Violence Center for helping women's voice be heard. Thank you also to Megan Quillinan and Holly LaTorre for making it all possible.

In closing, I must extend my deepest gratitude to Judy Brinkman of Life is 2 Short, my business coach. Her transformative workshop, "Open the Door to 24", was a beacon of illumination on my journey. Through her guidance and wisdom, I unearthed the dormant power within myself and discovered that I am indeed a force to be reckoned with. Judy, your impact on my life and the trajectory of my success is immeasurable, and I am forever thankful for that.

Without the help and support of these individuals, I would not have been able to navigate through these challenges and achieve my goals. Your kindness and assistance will always be remembered and appreciated.

Contents

Introduction: I am Maria Crowe. i

Chapter One: CONDEMNATION 1

Chapter Two: REFLECTION 12

Chapter Three: ADAPTATION 21

Chapter Four: BETRAYAL 27

Chapter Five: INJUSTICE........................... 53

Chapter Six: PERSECUTION 65

Chapter Seven: TRIAL 80

Chapter Eight: ISOLATION......................... 104

Chapter Nine: RESILIENCE......................... 117

Chapter Ten: VICTORY 147

Chapter Eleven: TRIUMPH 163

Chapter Twelve: ENDURANCE 181

Chapter Thirteen: TRANSFORMATION 213

Tips for Navigating the "Justice" System.............. 220

Tips for Dealing with a Narcissist 225

    Characteristics of a Narcissist in Divorce 225

    Navigating Divorce with a Narcissist 227

Journaling to a Positive Mindset 228

Author's Note....................................... 246

Author Bio 248

Introduction

I am Maria Crowe.

This is my story of a life interrupted, torn apart, and devastated.

More importantly, though, it is a story of personal triumph.

My story could just as easily be your story or anyone else's story, for that matter. Honestly, I did a lot of soul-searching before deciding whether or not to share what happened to me at the hands of a soul-less legal system, but I decided that if I could spare you, my reader, the heartache I suffered, it was all worth it.

For anyone dealing with something similar at the moment, I hope you will gain some useful insights – and inspiration.

Life often throws fastballs, and sometimes it throws hard curves. Some things you can control, but many others you cannot. The good news is that you can rewrite your story whenever you decide it is time. With patience, perseverance, passion, purpose, and prayer, you can re-write your story just as I have rewritten mine.

The past thirteen years have been a tumultuous rollercoaster ride, slinging me first to great heights and then dropping me to heartbreaking lows.

When I moved back to New York State from Cordova, I graduated from a highly regarded college and found work immediately as a professional broadcast journalist. I married the love of my life, settled into a comfortable home, and lovingly created three precious children.

As a working mom, I leveraged my skills to become an independent TV personality who focused almost exclusively on families. I was recognized by the President of the United States, the Governor of New York, and several other political and business leaders for my volunteer and fundraising efforts for the less fortunate.

I was also voted one of Willowbrook's most influential women and went on to be crowned National Miss for Crowns of Elegance, which remains one of my greatest honors. I was at the top of my game and completely naive to what was coming at me.

The storm that was to hit my life was not just a summer rainstorm offering a cool break from a heatwave. Instead, it would end up feeling like a Category 5 hurricane. It would devastate my career, take my freedom, ruin my reputation, and leave me without a physical home.

I can imagine that right now; you are thinking I must have committed some violent act or been caught dealing drugs or defrauding someone. What other crime would send me off in handcuffs in the back of a jail van on my way to a sterile jail cell?

I'm getting ahead of myself a bit here. I want to take you back to the beginning so that you can begin to get a clear picture of what precipitated this egregious injustice.

My life began to spiral out of control when I learned that my husband was committing adultery. It wasn't anything he admitted to right away. That took some digging to find out.

Everything started when he left one morning and didn't come home for dinner. I called, texted, and called again, but he didn't answer. I even called the local hospitals to make sure that he hadn't been in an accident. When I called his work, his secretary happily announced that he was out of the office for some rest and relaxation for a few days.

Very soon afterward, I realized that he had taken the electricity and cell phone out of his name. He also pulled nearly all the money from our joint account, leaving me to handle our expenses on one salary. I was so stressed out all the time that I could barely sleep. During the day, I walked around like a zombie because I was so tired. Twice, I ended up in the hospital as my body struggled from the stress.

I can't be sick, I thought—the kids.

As the door to the examination room screeched open, my heart jumped, and I shivered. But the doctor's face was relaxed, his light eyes warm.

"Good news, Mrs. Crowe. The biopsy came back as normal."

A rush of relief flooded through me until his next word.

"But..." he said.

His expression was serious as he noted my thin face and limbs. I had lost close to fifteen pounds.

"It's obvious that something is seriously wrong, Maria. You need to find a way to deal with the stress. Do some yoga. Go to the pool for a swim. A high-stress level is nothing to take lightly. This time, it was a false alarm. But next time..." He didn't finish his sentence but instead raised one eyebrow and tilted his head slightly.

I knew he was right. I had known it for a while, but it was his words that prompted me to go to a friend for a loan.

"I need to hire a private investigator. I will pay you back."

If you have been there, you know that divorce can be devastating, especially when you have young kids.

"But Mom, why did he leave us? Doesn't he love us anymore?"

How does a mother answer that question?

Where only weeks before, I had bounded out of bed excited for the day, now I woke up feeling exhausted, my pillow wet with tears, and my eyes red and bloodshot.

When I finally filed for divorce, events inexplicably descended into a nasty criminal case in which my cheating ex-husband hounded the State Police to arrest me on a bogus felony forgery charge.

The criminal case against me led me to a cataclysmic fall into the dark and rotting bowels of the New York State Supreme Court system. Ultimately, it landed me in the depravities of jail life, where my rose-colored glasses were torn from my face and obliterated on the rough concrete floor of my 4-foot x 12-foot jail cell.

Through my experience, I lost any belief in fairness in our justice system. The same attorneys, judges, and police officers that I had spent years lifting in my work turned a blind eye to the circumstances of my case. I watched helplessly as members of the media who, only weeks before, were my friends and colleagues, were now gleefully splashing my mug shot across every outlet, casting me as a criminal, without talking with me or even so much as asking me to comment on my behalf.

Through everything I was subjected to, I learned that what matters to those people is money, influence, connections, and looking good for the media. In other words, it appears to me that big egos matter and big egos stick together.

Since early 2011, I have appeared in court over three-hundred-sixty-five times in front of nine judges with fifteen different attorneys at my side. I have witnessed judicial conduct that would shock the most seasoned attorney.

I was forced to come up with nearly five hundred thousand dollars in legal representation and fees only to discover that finding someone willing to fight an insular system of judges and lawyers was nearly impossible.

Financially, I was broke. There was a point when I couldn't even afford to buy food or toilet paper for my kids. We were forced to move out of our home. Times got so desperate that I finally had no choice but to declare personal bankruptcy.

I am eager to share my story with you now—a story that separated me from my children and punitively awarded my ex-husband greater control over legal custody matters.

While my background as a reporter taught me to challenge injustices, I will be the first to admit that it did not prepare me for court battles, and it most especially did not prepare me for jail life.

Before I found myself handcuffed and escorted out of the courthouse toward a jail cell, I had never even received a speeding ticket.

Throughout the ordeal, people I thought were my friends deserted me. I could only assume that, after reading the news of my arrest, they didn't want to be associated with a "criminal," which was understandable. But not one of them called me to get my side of the story.

On the day of the verdict, as the guard handcuffed and escorted me to jail, I was in a state of total disbelief. It didn't feel real. Honestly, I finally felt at peace. It couldn't get any worse.

It was a relief to know that I had hit rock bottom.

At least that's what I thought.

But then things got worse.

Chapter One

CONDEMNATION

"The ultimate measure of a man is not where he stands in moments of comfort and convenience, but where he stands at times of challenge and controversy."

~Martin Luther King, Jr.

May 17, 2016, will forever be burned in my memory. That was the day my life changed forever.

"What's your verdict?" the judge asked, his face stony, his mouth tight.

"Guilty," the jury foreman stated, his words sending a thundering reverberation across the courtroom.

Suddenly, it was as though I was out of my body observing myself. For weeks, I had been crying. I had cried an ocean as the jury was selected and then another as I sat in disbelief while testimonies were made. It came to the point that I felt there were no more tears left to cry. You would think that with a verdict of guilty, I would have been tearful, angry, infuriated, or even hopeless. But instead, I suddenly felt like I was being lifted up by something much bigger and more powerful than me.

You may think I'm crazy or that I am not being honest about what I was feeling at that moment. But

I'm telling you the absolute truth. I experienced a full-blown spiritual moment that left me feeling loved, guided, and ready to handle whatever came next.

The trip to the jail in the back of the van felt almost surreal.

The accompanying officers considered me in the rearview mirror, one appearing as though he wanted to say something. When he finally spoke, his expression was earnest.

"Ma'am, I'm paid not to talk to you during this trip, but I can't keep my mouth shut. I hope you don't mind me saying that you need to fight this. I have never witnessed anything like it before. Something isn't right here. This is wrong."

When we arrived at the jail, the corrections officer was neither kind nor brusque.

"I need all your personal possessions, ma'am."

I slowly removed the sapphire ring and a pair of gold sapphire earrings I had purchased for myself years earlier, as well as a faith bracelet that a good friend had loaned me for luck during the court proceedings. I couldn't look at the officer as I placed each one in the pouch and sealed the top.

His next words brought me back to reality.

"I need your shoes," he said matter-of-factly.

My eyes lifted and found his. They were a deep, soft brown.

"My shoes?" I asked, feeling at first confused and then explosively angry. My ex had taken everything from me—my kids, my home, my money, my freedom, and my smile. And now he was getting my shoes.

I glanced at the high-heeled Etienne Aigner heels I had worn to court that day.

The officer was patient as a terrifying anxiety attack caused an onslaught of tears. I released the left shoe first, then the right, and then bent to pick them up and place them in the bag.

This is really happening, I thought. He is even getting my shoes.

I was crying so hard I could barely get my next words out.

"Can I make a phone call?"

The officer's eyes were kind when he indicated the phone on his desk. I lifted the phone to my ear, but my mind was blank.

518..637...or is it 367. Damn it, I thought, panic overtaking me as I tried to recall his number.

I needed to center myself, so I closed my eyes and pulled in a deep breath. Once I felt calm, I dialed.

"Hello." The voice was deep and husky. I immediately knew I had dialed the wrong number and hung up.

Hands shaking, I turned to the officer whose eyes were kind.

"Go ahead and try again," he said.

This time, when the phone connected, I spoke without a greeting.

"Alain, get me the fuck out of here. Please!" I said, a deep sob heaving my chest, tears sopping the front of the county-issued drab green shirt.

"Mar, look, calm down. I'm coming right over with your cousin."

I glanced at the officer to see if I had more time. His voice was kind when he said, "Take as long as you need." Relieved, I turned my attention back to Alain.

When the call was completed, I was handcuffed and shackled around my waist and feet before being escorted down a long hallway. The metal doors were huge. A mechanical voice warned, "Open 1, 2, 3," followed by a slam and the sound of the doors lock, lock, locking as I shuffled closer to the hellish nightmare that had become my life with only one word.

Guilty.

Everything inside the jail was a dull gray, almost like a nursing home, but colder.

Two huge metal doors opened at the end of the hall, and a tall, muscular female officer greeted me with a pretty smile.

"Don't worry, you will be okay," she assured me. "Just be careful. They bite."

Across the room, women were sitting at various tables, looking curiously in our direction. Some were big and looked tough, while others appeared almost shrunken. The scene reminded me of a bad day on the playground.

I dropped my eyes, thinking, *I'm going to get my ass kicked.*

A feeling of cold dread crept up my spine. These women were not the type I generally hung out with over Saturday morning coffee. I was too scared to make eye contact with anyone, so I hugged my belongings close and looked down, crying.

At this point, I had no idea how long I would be there. I was sent to jail without bail, and the judge decided I was a flight risk because my parents lived in Cordova.

Inspecting the 4-foot x 12-foot space took only one quick glance. The place had a cold smell, but it wasn't horrible. The small window over the bed was narrow, barely a sliver, allowing very light to come through.

I stared at the jail-issued belongings that would be mine for the foreseeable future. I had been given one blanket, two pairs of boxer shorts, one small tube of toothpaste and a toothbrush, one roll of toilet paper, one jail rape elimination pamphlet, two-bed sheets, one inmate handbook (that I would need to return), one pillowcase, one bar of soap, one drinking cup, one bath towel, one pair of oversized men's socks, one well-worn sports bra, and one thin nightgown. I was also issued a green shirt made from a stiff, unbreathable fabric. At least the green pants weren't that bad.

I will never forget the sound of the black Crocs flopping against the jail floors, reminding me daily that he even got my shoes.

On the first day, I learned about "classification." This is where inmates are evaluated based on their medical, mental, and criminal history. The guards tested each new inmate before letting them "loose" into the general population. I ended up locked in classification longer because my body had such a bad reaction to the TB shot that was issued on my first day.

Looking around the small cell, I noticed a stainless-steel toilet, a sink, a bunk with a plastic green mattress, and a pillow made of a plastic tarp that was so well-used it laid completely flat on the mattress. The gray cement walls were clean, but it felt really cold.

Shivering, I cried with no thought of what the other inmates might think about me. I was freaking out that I might be there for seven years. The thought that I would miss my kids growing up started another panic attack, and I literally got down on my knees to pray.

"God, I'm not mad at you. I know there's a devil, and this is him trying to get me to hate you," I said.

I thought about the Book of Job. I don't like to admit it, but at that moment, I hated my ex so intensely that I had no words. I had never hated anyone and was shocked at the depth of emotion. I wanted to kick something and lash out in a million different ways, but I was afraid.

"Why is this happening?" I cried. I was a good person. I had done nothing wrong.

When the order came to go to bed, I curled up in a ball on the stiff bed and tried to sleep. But the lights never went out, so each time I began to doze off, I was startled awake. I later learned that the lights were always on so the guards could see the inmates, making it more difficult for anyone to kill themselves.

During my time in jail, I learned that others control when you sleep, eat, wash yourself, and even contact others. There is no freedom. None.

At 7:30 each morning, we were woken by a guard yelling at the top of their lungs.

"Count!"

We were treated like cattle as we were herded to breakfast and then back to our cells.

We were expected to jump up and stand in front of our cells during shift changes so incoming officers could count the inmates to ensure no one had committed suicide or, worse, escaped. After the count was complete, once more, we were assaulted by another even louder yell.

"Clear!"

(Every day of my incarceration, I thought, *We're not deaf. We can hear you.*)

After another few minutes, another guard would shout, "Chow!" I had no idea what the word meant, so I asked another inmate.

"That is how they refer to mealtime," she explained.

It all felt so degrading. We weren't animals. We were human beings who somehow ended up in a terrible situation.

Some officers liked to entertain themselves by blowing piercing whistles in the morning. Waking up to that eardrum-splitting sound literally hurt, especially since the sound bounced off the concrete walls, making it feel even more piercing.

Sometimes, after breakfast, we were allowed to go outdoors for an hour; other days, we weren't allowed out until after dinner, and some days, not at all. It depended on the officer on duty and their mood.

Lunch was served each day at 11:30 AM and dinner at 4:30 PM.

From 2:30 PM to 4:00 PM, the jail officers accepted new inmates, forcing us into lockdown. Around 4:00 PM, they opened the cell doors to conduct another headcount, and we were allowed to come out of our cells again.

It was the job of the officer on duty to summon us from our individual tables into a single line. We were entitled to select one meal, one beverage, and a "spork," a combination of a fork and spoon.

The routine was the same every day—thirty minutes to eat. When we finished, an officer checked each utensil to ensure they were returned to the kitchen making it impossible for anything to be used as a weapon. Then, medications were distributed at 6:00 PM. I was the only inmate not on medication.

We were allowed to use the telephone from 9:00 AM until 11:00 AM, 1:00 PM to 3:45 PM, and again from 6:00 PM to 11:30 PM. The jail guards conducted yet another headcount at midnight each night. If anyone had fallen asleep in the meantime, they were expected to get up with everyone else and stand in front of their cells. All doors were locked until wake-up time, when the routine started all over.

The first few nights, I couldn't sleep. My mind raced as I tried to get comfortable on a metal board attached to a concrete wall. What they called a pillow was flatter than a Saltine cracker, and it crackled, sounding like the tarp that made up its surface. The space was freezing, even though it was late May, and I couldn't get used to sleeping with the lights on.

The chairs in the shared space were hard and cold and attached to the tables. Those in the TV area were heavy and no warmer.

Watching television in the general area was nearly impossible because everyone was so loud.

"Can you turn it down?" I once asked in frustration.

"Hey, this is the way we like it," one woman bitched back. A few of the other women got involved, and we ended up in lockdown.

The majority of inmates only quieted down during lockdown hours. Plus, they only really cared to watch shows about jail or drugs. Maybe they thought that was cool, but it made no sense to me.

The only liquids we were allowed were water or Kool-Aid, and then that was only at lunch or dinner. Meals consisted of bread, bread, and more bread, making me wonder if the kitchen was supplied with a free, limitless supply of white bread.

There was toast for breakfast. Lunch consisted of bologna sandwiches, peanut butter and jelly sandwiches, cheese, and bread. Dinner was usually a huge portion of something plopped on our plates, and occasionally, we were lucky enough to get pudding for dessert.

Laundry days were on Tuesdays and Thursdays. At 8:00 AM sharp, we were handed a fishnet laundry bag labeled with our cell number. We weren't afforded the luxury of Downy or dryer sheets, so the clothes usually came out wrinkled and smelly.

We could request a razor to shave our legs from 9:00 AM to 10:00 AM. Usually, I tried to get a hold of one on Tuesdays and Saturdays before family visits, if only to make myself feel more normal.

After the visits, jail guards checked us for contraband. We were made to strip naked and then squat and cough at the same time. I cried every single time. The practice was so humiliating.

We were also able to request a nail clipper at 9:00 AM. Since the jail only had one clipper, all the inmates shared the same one. The idea was so nasty that I preferred to use my teeth and did exactly that when my nails got too long.

On the upside, I participated regularly in religious services. Volunteers came from area churches, and the Jehovah's Witnesses came to study the bible with us. Most of the women went only to escape the routine of the jail, but I found great comfort in the words and thoughts presented. I was a woman of faith. I would not let these terrible circumstances change that. I hung on to every word and took uplifting phrases back to my cold cell.

Inmates could draw money from a jail commissary. Family and friends placed money in accounts that would allow inmates to purchase snacks, clothes, stationery, toothpaste, and other essentials. I generally bought stamps, envelopes, and other small items.

All incoming mail was opened and inspected. During mail call, our name was called, and we were expected to stand in front of the officer as they opened the envelope. One of the officers confided that the male inmates often received naked pictures from their girlfriends. There was no privacy whatsoever, and the staff seemed to enjoy the process a lot.

The only things I looked forward to were visits from friends and family—and hot showers. The water running over my exhausted body melted the muscles that had grown tight around my shoulders and hips from trying to sleep on the hard jail bed. I locked myself under the falling water for as long as needed. Standing under the running water helped clear my mind, so it was the one and only place I was able to find any peace.

Because I was the only inmate not on meds or considered a suicide risk, I was allowed to take a shower upstairs, which meant I had the shower all to myself. Since it was on the same level as the officer's tower, I was careful to be sure no one could see me inside, naked.

On the first evening locked behind bars, I sat on the stone-cold bunk bubbling with hot anger. By then, I thought I had no more tears, but a fresh onslaught overtook me, and I couldn't stop.

"Why is this happening to me, God? I am a good person. I don't deserve any of this. How am I going to survive without my kids?"

Tears rained over my cheeks as desperation tore through my body and panic raced through my limbs. The pain in my head grew stronger and stronger.

"Stop crying," I ordered myself quietly. "You're only making it worse."

I thought about the maximum seven-year jail sentence I faced. My kids were only ten, twelve, and thirteen. I would completely miss their formative years.

"This isn't happening," I said, pounding my leg.

When my ex-husband left us, I thought my heart was shattered. But at that moment, sitting on that hard bunk in a cold cell, I wished I could tear my own heart out of my chest. I didn't want it anymore. It hurt too much, and it was destroying me. How could I live without my kids?

I got down on my knees for the second time that day. I am a faith-full woman. Yes, I was angry and disappointed, but I was not angry at God. With my knees burning against the concrete, I began to pray.

"God, you know I don't blame you for any of this. I am willing to do what you ask. But please don't take me away from my kids. I can't breathe without them."

I have no idea how long I stayed in the kneeling position. Because I could feel God with me in that space, I didn't want to move. I must have fallen asleep because suddenly I heard the guard shouting.

"Count!"

Mornings bled into days and another night. Then it happened.

"Maria Crowe, you've got a letter."

I jumped to my feet as the officer opened the mail, lifted an eyebrow, and handed the contents to me.

I tore open the official-looking document and stared at once, disbelieving and not at all surprised. I was being served papers. My ex-husband, who was earning one-hundred-fifty-two-thousand dollars annually, had already applied to the court to stop all child support payments.

He was not petitioning the courts to get custody of our kids. He didn't want the kids. This was all about money. He was even darker and sicker than I had initially given him credit for.

Chapter Two

REFLECTION

"The only way to do great work is to love what you do."

~Steve Jobs

The days passed slowly. I was used to being busy and needed something to do.

Thankfully, just when I was almost at wit's end, an officer I recognized from check-in opened the cell door to conduct an inspection.

After she looked around, I tentatively asked, "Can I please have paper and a pen? Or a book?" I wasn't sure about jail etiquette, so I hoped what I was asking would not make her angry.

"Let me see what I can do," she answered with a smile. She was pretty with bright blue eyes and light brown hair. I noticed that she smelled good and wore makeup.

The pretty guard returned a little while later with her arms full. She handed me a pack of cookies, a pen, a pencil, coloring pencils, coloring pages, shampoo, and conditioner.

"I went around, and here's what the girls wanted you to have," the guard said. "They are actually pretty cool. It's not that bad here, really."

For the first time in what seemed like ages, I smiled. God was still listening.

I made myself busy with the coloring. After 30 minutes or so, I moved on to reading.

During the first week in jail, I spent a lot of time thinking. My mind traveled back to beautiful times, growing up with loving, old-school parents, working as a professional journalist, and marrying the man of my dreams.

My parents, Adam and Claire Ferreira, were born and raised in Nazare, Western Cordova. On Valentine's Day in 1971, they immigrated to Falls Rivers, MA, where my mom's parents lived. Neither one of them spoke English at the time.

My older brother Paulo had been born in Cordova. I was born in Springdale, Massachusetts, a medium-sized city in western Massachusetts, just north of the Connecticut state line. My parents worked at Riverside Manufacturing Works in Springdale alongside my mom's family, producing American sporting equipment – mostly basketballs and golf balls.

When I was seven, my paternal grandfather fell ill, compelling my parents to move us to Nazare in Cordova so they could care for him. In a fun and memorable twist, my maternal grandparents joined us. They lived within walking distance from my parents, so I bounced around, spending happy nights with both.

Growing up in my family, it felt like everyone was related. I became known as the precocious 'American girl.' I loved our big family, and I especially loved being my grandparents' princess.

I remember helping my grandfather put on his socks. To me, he had "best friend" energy, always happy and whistling.

I found myself smiling when I thought about my mom telling me that a woman needed to learn how to sew so she could stitch her husband's socks. I could only imagine myself saying this to my daughters today—they would laugh me right off the planet!

At one point, my dad opened a butcher shop, and from then on, we ate a lot of steaks. I don't know why the memory caused my eyes to mist. Maybe it was because both my parents worked so hard to give us a good life.

My preteen years were typical 'girly girl' years. I played with Barbies, learned to cook and sew, played sports in school, and rode my bike.

Around the same time, everything shifted for me. I was thirteen when I had a forever pivotal moment.

One afternoon, a religious education teacher asked our class what each wanted to be when they grew up. I felt proud to stand up and share my desire to become a fashion designer.

"It's my dream to become famous and make lots of money," I added with a happy smile.

After the teacher had heard from everyone, she turned back to me, and in front of the entire class, she called me selfish.

"You are the only child in this room who is not considering a profession geared toward helping others," she admonished.

That moment completely changed me. I began focusing on what I wanted to do with my life. My grandfather used to say that I would make a good attorney because I was organized, and I liked to debate. But I hated the idea of being stuck in an office, confined to a space devoid of natural light.

As time went on, I developed an interest in news reporting. I loved watching the news on television and grew super curious about current events. It was during this time that I decided I would like to work as a broadcast journalist. I enjoyed telling stories that could have a positive influence on others, so it seemed like a good fit for me.

When my brother turned eighteen, he returned to America and got married. I remained in Cordova through high school, and my parents were intent on sending me to the University of Cordova. It was especially important to them that I attend college since neither of them had had the opportunity to do so.

After graduating from high school, I waved goodbye as I left for a solo flight that would take me to see my brother in the United States.

"You should stay here," he said, noting all the opportunities to study broadcast journalism on the East Coast.

"Here as in the US?" I asked.

"Why not? There are great opportunities here, especially on the East Coast."

When I arrived in the US, I came with one hundred dollars and a couple of summer outfits. There was no question in my mind that both my parents and grandparents would not approve of me staying, but I also knew that my brother was right. I believed in myself enough to know that I could take this chance on myself, so I called my parents.

"I've decided to stay here," I announced. I was ready to pursue my dream, and I believed in myself. I could do this.

My parents had been devastated. In fact, my mom was so angry that she refused to speak to me for three months. But I knew she'd come around.

I buckled down quickly and got to work. I would prove to them that staying in the US was the right decision for me. Plus, I was sure I could slay college.

As a teen in Cordova, though, I had never worked a steady job, and now I was responsible for coming up with the cost of not only a college education. I also needed to come up with living expenses. I would need to hustle.

And hustle was exactly what I did.

Because I was still waiting for my transcripts from Cordova and didn't want to waste any time, I decided to sign up for Fall classes at a local college before finding a waitressing job where I would wait tables and manage catering events at a Cordovan Restaurant.

It turned out I was a bit naïve about what it would actually cost to go to school, though. I had no understanding of the cost differences between a private and public college until I applied. So, I started at a public school and applied to Cityscape Institute, a private school known for producing successful journalists. Cityscape accepted me for the Spring term, but with only a five-hundred-dollar scholarship, I would need to come up with thirteen thousand dollars to register.

I took out loans and borrowed some money from my uncle to meet my tuition and board expenses. In January of 1998, I walked through the doors of Cityscape to start the next phase of the adventure.

The opportunities offered there were incredible. I interned at television stations in the surrounding area and was among five students who founded River Rock Radio in Harborview, a station that grew into the number one college television news station in the northeast.

We were news geeks, living and breathing current events. We covered news at the college, but we also took on serious national topics. While working with our team, I also reported the news for Echo Vibe FM, Cityscape's radio station. If that wasn't enough for me to do, I joined the soccer team.

At Cityscape, we were lucky enough to learn from one of the best, most hard-to-please instructors,

Marsha Della Justina, who instinctively knew how to prepare students with the multi-tasking skills required to succeed in modern newsrooms. I stepped up to every challenge and was thrilled when the Associated Press endowed me with an award for coverage of a fire in Harborview.

With Dean's List honors and a Who's Who in American Universities and Colleges under my belt, I proudly walked across the stage at our graduation ceremony. I was sad that my parents couldn't attend, but thrilled when I got their call to congratulate me.

"We're so proud of you, honey," my mom said making my heart feel even fuller.

To make things even better, I immediately landed a job as a news producer and assignment editor at a Vista Broadcast affiliate in my birth town of Springsdale, Massachusetts. I had only been on staff for a couple of months when a major fatal car crash sent me reaching out to the media spokesperson for the State Police.

"I'm Darius Crowe," he offered.

We didn't speak often at first, and honestly, he struck me as being rather pompous. As his assignment editor, I found him hard to work with.

While Darius initially put me off, I soon realized that we shared many things in common. We were both ambitious. We had a similar love of family, plus we were passionate about our careers.

It was the Thanksgiving of 2000 when Darius and I coincidentally were scheduled to work. After a nice conversation with him, I recall thinking, *"Hmm, he's actually a nice person."*

Soon afterward, Darius asked me out, and it wasn't long before we spent as much time together as possible. I often heard about feeling butterflies in the stomach, but this was my first experience of feeling it myself. We enjoyed going to musicals, and we discussed moving to Metropolis Heights.

But destiny intervened.

It's positive, I thought, as I stared at the pregnancy test in my hand. Everything changed quickly.

Darius's parents lived in Riverside Grove, and with a child on the way, we wanted to move closer to them. We hatched a plan to relocate to their area, which was home to multiple stations in a solid market.

It wasn't long before we both received offers. Darius was hired at a local barracks in New York, and I accepted an exciting opportunity with a new 24-hour news station that would be called Capital News 11. I would be an assistant news director working with a team of journalists.

The concept of a 24-hour news station excited me since it was a new concept at the time.

"I need to be honest," I said at my interview. "I am two months pregnant."

"Congratulations! We don't let events like this get in the way when we have a candidate like you. When would you like to start?"

Working there was an amazing experience. To be on the ground floor of a new station, especially a station that was forward-thinking enough to produce a product that didn't previously exist.

My passion for the news exploded with this incredible opportunity, and I had the good fortune to be working when a high-powered storm moved through our area. As the assistant news director, I was stationed in the control room with the anchor while coordinating five "live" reporters in the field. The big bosses watched from the newsroom as we unleashed all the bells and whistles.

"Darius, it was amazing!" I gushed over dinner that night. "I was managing everyone, and we were writing material on the fly. I didn't know if it was possible with all those "lives" back-to-back, but we killed it!"

"I'm not surprised, honey," he had said. "You're damned good at what you do."

Both of our careers were budding. The move had been a good decision.

One day, Darius's father surprised us by asking if we were planning to marry.

Darius glanced at me, smiled, and said, "Yes, we are."

I was grinning from ear to ear. I was already blessed on so many levels, and life was only getting better.

I flew to Cordova to share the news with my parents, and on my return, Darius met me in a limousine at the airport.

"I want my future bride to ride in style," he said. "Maria Ferreira, will you do me the honor of becoming my wife?"

"Yes," I answered in a serious tone. Then, I laughed and said, "Yes!"

A soft rain blessed our union with good luck. Butterflies fluttered in my stomach as I proclaimed my love for Darius Crowe before my entire family.

"Do you take this woman to be your lawfully wedded wife?"

"I sure do," he had responded eagerly.

Only a handful of the wedding attendees knew I was four months pregnant.

The party was amazing as everyone danced and laughed. Even though the deejay forgot our favorite song, a friend came to the rescue, "Hold on! I've got that CD in my car!"

Exhausted at the end of the night, we fell into bed and made love for the first time as Mr. and Mrs. Crowe.

After living in Cascade Falls for just over a year, we finally purchased a four-bedroom home on Maplewood Lane in Clifton Meadows. Life was perfect.

Never in a billion years could I have imagined that only a few short years later, I would be in jail at the hands of the same man.

Chapter Three

ADAPTATION

"Life is 10% what happens to you and 90% how you react to it."

~Charles R. Swindol

I was in Willowbrook County jail for about a week before I started to make acquaintances and establish routines. It was right around that same time when we were forced into lockdown.

We learned that an inmate had been causing problems, and the guards wanted to keep a closer eye on her.

The inmate flipped out, screaming, "You just want to rape me when I'm sleeping!"

It made me sad to see her so upset. She was someone the other inmates didn't like to be around, so she always ate alone. She made a big deal about not wearing a bra because she believed bras caused cancer.

At the end of the lockdown, I dragged my belongings to Cell 113, which was to be my new area. Glancing around, I saw something on the floor and bent down to inspect it.

Is that blood? I thought, feeling a creepy crawling up my spine.

I called over a corrections officer.

"Is that blood?" I asked, pointing to the floor.

"I don't think so," she responded after bending down to take a closer look. But she was happy to get me disinfectant so I could scrub the floor to be absolutely sure.

My new cell was adjacent to a woman who had dreadful nightmares every night. She often woke me up with her moans and strange noises.

The poor thing. I wonder what happened to her, I thought.

I was beginning to become accustomed to the idiosyncrasies of the facility and the confusing personalities when I heard from my attorney with news that caused my anxiety to reach a fever pitch.

"I'm sorry, Maria, but your bail hearing will be moved out a few days," he said.

"Why?" I asked, my emotions skipping between anger and frustration.

"It's out of my control," he said after telling me the bail hearing that I hoped would occur on Friday had instead been scheduled for the following Tuesday, after the Memorial Day holiday weekend.

"But that's the same day I am scheduled to appear in family court for Darius's petition to stop paying child-support payments," I said.

"I know," he said. "It's not a problem. There is plenty of time between hearings."

I felt angry, frustrated, sad, vulnerable, and honestly, completely powerless, sitting there in a jail cell facing a lengthy jail sentence for a crime I DID NOT commit. A sweet corrections officer tried to comfort me, which I appreciated, but I had to release the despair that had me feeling terrified, so I poured it all out in my journal.

Thankfully, I had lots of time to write. I wrote about everything and anything. Imagine yourself sitting in jail while the media plasters you all over the newspapers and television, portraying you as a criminal when you know you did absolutely nothing wrong.

I hate that my kids are being put through all of this. Who am I without them? I might as well be dead, I wrote.

The DA is threatening me with up to seven years behind bars. She knows this was a divorce case. And why is it okay for Darius to sign and deposit insurance checks made out to both of us, but I'm forced to sit in this place, being treated like a criminal and feeling like my heart is broken? It makes no sense to me. I was arrested, prosecuted, and sent to jail without bail. It all feels crazy. What kind of system is this, anyway?

By now, I was scribbling out of pure frustration.

My relationship with God was my only comfort. I had always heard it said that you must forgive those who do you wrong. Almost daily, I would open to the Book of Job in the Bible, reminding myself that if he could handle everything that happened to him, I could, too.

I tried to pray for Darius. I really did. I had forgiven him before, but this was a much more difficult betrayal to wrap my head around.

During the empty hours, I colored birds and flowers and then glued them with toothpaste to the cell's dreary walls. I made a calendar for myself so I wouldn't lose track of the days of the week or how long I had been there.

Nearly all the inmates I met were repeat offenders, serving at least a second sentence. With lots of time on my hands, I asked them questions to learn about their lives and what landed them in the Willowbrook County jail. To make myself feel better, I pretended I was an undercover reporter on a special assignment who, through exhaustive research, learned that most of the crimes included driving while intoxicated, drug use and/or possession, theft, and sex crimes. I learned that most of the women inmates had committed crimes against children.

One afternoon during my first week in confinement, an officer handed me a box of cookies from a woman who was a known child molester. Not wanting to offend anyone, I took the cookies but was happy to pass them on to an inmate who came in for a cocaine overdose and said she was hungry. I wrote her a note.

Thank you so much for the cookies. I appreciate your kindness even though I don't agree with what you did. As a mother, I find the idea of molesting a child horrific, but it is not my job to judge. That judgment is only for God to make.

As the days went by, I heard that one of the inmates who was convicted of sexually assaulting a child had received a seven-year prison sentence—the same length of time with which I was being threatened.

Are you kidding me? I could be here for the same length of time as a convicted child molester? That's insanity. Where is the fairness in this system? I raged into my journal.

I became very ill from a tuberculosis shot I was administered in jail, causing a brutal migraine and a painful red blotch on my arm. I felt panicked, fearing I would be given meds that might drug me or even kill me. But needing medical care, I sat alongside two other women inmates, one of them barely twenty years old.

"I like heroin a lot," she explained when I asked her why she was in. "I'm addicted to it. I've been here three times already, and twice I've been in prison."

Her tone was casual—as if her incarcerations were just another day at the beach. She also admitted that she had even gotten caught selling drugs in jail.

"You SOLD drugs in here?" I asked, both shocked and laughing at the same time.

"Yes, my boyfriend would come see me and bring them to me, and then I would sell them here," she said with a shrug.

I honestly felt like I had somehow been cast in a bad movie. I had never even seen heroin, but for her, heroin was her life.

My ping pong partner, a tall, leggy woman, shared that she was serving jail time for her fifth DWI. I couldn't wrap my head around how this was possible. She spoke so intelligently. How could someone like her have fallen into such a preventable addiction?

Another young, fit woman with long, pretty hair who didn't like to hang out with the other girls confided that her boyfriend had punched her in the face.

"I was only defending myself," she said when she admitted that she had thrown a picture frame at him, which had cut his leg. He had called the police on her, and she was taken into custody. He was not.

Her story incited something in me, and I got angry.

"How is that possible? What happened?" I asked.

She explained that she had been on probation for a DWI conviction at the time the boyfriend assaulted her. When the police arrived, they handcuffed her and then placed her under arrest before she could explain the circumstances.

"Even if you were on probation, I just don't understand why a Judge would protect an abuser," I said.

"She arrived here with a black eye and bruises," a corrections officer said, corroborating the woman's story, adding with a shrug, "Sometimes the system works against you."

This poor abused woman had been sentenced to eight months in jail. Her abuser was walking around free, living his life like he had done nothing wrong.

I met a new inmate who introduced herself while I was sitting reading. She told me that her mother's boyfriend had begun raping her when she was six years old. At around age thirteen, she learned from a television show that what the man had been doing for years was wrong.

"My mom didn't want to press charges against him because she didn't want to be single with three kids," she explained.

She said that because of the abuse, she couldn't let anyone touch her or even get close.

"I guess it doesn't matter because my ovaries have been damaged from the abuse," she added.

I struggled to keep from crying, and I thought my heart would break for her. That guy was a monster. Why was HE not in jail? Where was the justice?

While most of the inmates were friendly and engaging, others could be catty or even downright mean. Some referred to me as "Smiley" or "Cinderella."

"That one over there eavesdrops on your phone conversations," one woman said, tilting her head in the direction of a dark-haired woman sitting comfortably across the room. "Apparently, 'Miss Gossip' likes to get the scoop on everyone," she said.

I had no idea she had been listening in since she hadn't so much as said boo to me since I had been there.

Some women tried to start fights over silly stuff, like a song. One night, I was playing ping pong while all the other girls were sitting together watching the BET Awards. Believe it or not, I almost forgot I was in jail for a moment. But then, an argument erupted over one of the songs, and the officer turned off the TV.

End of story.

Chapter Four

BETRAYAL

"The truth is everyone is going to hurt you. You just got to find the ones worth suffering for."

~Bob Marley

When you're traveling on a straight, smooth path, it's easy to lose focus and take your eyes off the road. I will admit that when it came to my marriage, I was completely and totally oblivious to the oncoming tractor-trailer headed straight for me.

Darius and I had settled into a happy, successful life in Clifton Meadows when, one day, I received a call from the operator of my son's daycare facility.

"But don't worry, your son is OK," the director said soothingly.

We couldn't get a straight answer from the daycare about what happened to our 18-month-old son. But that night, the incident was the top story on all the local newscasts, and our family was smack dab in the middle of it all.

The newscaster's expression was serious when she reported that our young son had pushed open a door, wandered outside the daycare building, and was preparing to crawl across Ridge Highway—one of the busiest, most hectic roads in the Valley—when a couple saw him and jumped out of their vehicle to save the day.

The operators of the center deflected questions, but the couple that rescued my son called Channel 15 to report what happened.

"The whole incident was shocking, just shocking," the man said into the microphone while shaking his head sadly.

"We're so grateful we noticed him," his wife added. "Can you imagine what would have happened to that little boy if we hadn't been there?" she asked, her eyes misting at the thought.

The state conducted an investigation and issued the center a significant fine. I, on the other hand, emerged from the experience in "mama grizzly" mode. After several deep conversations, Darius suggested I leave my TV career to focus on raising our kids since, by then, our second child was on the way.

Only a few months after leaving my career, Darius suggested I get a part-time job. I quickly found a job in academia, teaching communications at a local college and a broadcast journalism school called the Radio and TV Institute, located just a few miles away from our home.

Soon after, a news director called and asked if I would be interested in joining their team at Channel 18, an NBC affiliate in Riverside Valley.

"I don't know, Maria. I think it's better if you stay out of the TV business," Darius said when I asked what he thought about the opportunity.

"But Darius, you know how much I love it. Plus, it opens up opportunities for other options," I said.

He wasn't thrilled when I decided to go ahead and take the TV job, so I was careful about my hours at first. I continued teaching, and within a year, I was working full-time.

"I'm relieved you're making money again, honey," he said one morning while we were getting ready for work.

"Me, too, Darius. But I miss the kids when I'm away from the house," I said. "I am really struggling with the idea that a bad person could have taken our little guy. I would have never recovered from that. What do you think about getting them into a private preschool facility? It would probably be easier than worrying about the babysitter not showing up."

With Darius so busy in his career and me working three part-time jobs, we decided to register the kids in Willowbrook Academy, a private school.

Our third child—a second daughter—entered the world shortly afterward. Darius had attended Lamaze classes with me, so he coached me through the birth.

"You're doing amazing," the midwife soothed as my daughter's head crowned. "Only a few more pushes, and you'll be good to go."

"Honey, I'm so proud of you. Just keep breathing. You're doing great," Darius had whispered in my ear.

As a couple, we were making good money and achieving our dreams, including building our family and creating three beautiful, happy, and healthy children.

"We are so blessed," I said one evening after kissing the kids goodnight and settling onto the couch next to Darius.

"That's a fact. We certainly are," he agreed softly before closing his eyes and touching his lips to mine.

As the kids grew, I loved teaching Sunday School at our church and volunteering often at the kids' school. I also loved my work, but after a few years, private school costs virtually outweighed what I was making. We had several difficult discussions about who would leave their career to stay home.

"I honestly don't want to leave my career. I love my work," Darius said.

"But I love mine, too," I countered. "Plus, I have the opportunity to make more money than you are making if I take the news director position."

After multiple discussions, I meditated on what was most important to me. Yes, I loved my job, but I loved being a mom more. I brought my kids into the world because I believed I could raise good humans, and I knew that as good as I was at my job, I was even better at being a mom. Plus, I was always someone who didn't need much to be happy. So, if it was better for the kids that I be home, I would be there for them.

"Okay, Darius, I guess you're right," I said after another long talk. "It's nice to be out of the house creating cool things, but I really miss the kids when I'm working, especially when I have to work late."

Memories flitted through my mind—afternoons at the park, lying on the grass and watching the clouds skitter by as the kids darted around laughing. Sitting under the trees, braiding my little girls' hair, and later removing a tick from my son's private parts. (That memory made me smile. The poor kid was mortified!) Creating Halloween costumes, removing a random bug from my daughter's eyes, and Saturday afternoon crafts. There was so much I loved about having children in my life.

"I know it's hard for you to leave them," Darius said with a smile. "It's hard for me, too. They're such good kids." (Never in a million years would I have guessed that six months later, not only would he leave me, but he would leave them, too.)

With the decision made, I settled into raising my kids full-time. Always the creative, though, ideas continually flowed into my mind. While pushing my kids on the swing at the park or walking through the mall on our way to an afternoon movie, my mind would wander to creating something that combined my two passions—family and media.

A spark of an idea ignited into a full-blown vision, and finally, I could no longer keep it to myself.

"I want to create a half-hour television show called *Family Matters.* It would be dedicated fully to parenting. What do you think?" I asked over morning coffee.

The show would be intended to help families build healthy relationships and act as a "survival guide" for parents. As it came together, the fast-paced format featured interviews with experts, doctors, and psychologists. Each episode was broken into five topics and a "Question of the Week" segment, in which we often interviewed random local parents.

I shot footage for *"Family Matters"* in Willowbrook's High School television studio, and as we grew, we included footage from the surrounding area. The show grew quickly; soon, I could hire a reporter to help with the writing and shooting. Together, we combined segments from the studio with shots captured in the field. It was a blast.

One evening, after the kids were tucked into bed, I said, "I received the nicest note today, and I've been getting quite a few like this. It says, 'This show is so relatable. I feel like you get me.'"

Darius smiled. "You're doing good work, honey."

"Thanks," I said, feeling myself glow from the inside. I was doing good work, and it felt wonderful.

The show launched and immediately became popular. I could barely contain my excitement.

One morning, over breakfast, I shared my idea for taking the program national.

"What do you think?" I asked, barely able to contain my excitement.

"That's great. Look at you, getting more popular than me, Maria." I couldn't tell if he was happy or envious, but he seemed supportive.

I was so happy. Everything that I had always hoped for was coming to fruition. I was so proud that I was creating it all while still maintaining my full-time mom status. It was the perfect scenario. Sure, sometimes things came up that were challenging, but I realized obstacles can be life's best teachers. I was not a quitter.

During that time, I founded Unity Bonds Initiative, a nonprofit arm of the *Family Matters* brand, to attract sponsorships and raise funding for area families. The organization and its name were inspired by my parents, who had been married for fifty-three years, and a conversation with philanthropist Doris Buffet, who said, "Mrs. Crowe, I am impressed with what you are creating. I just gave Bill Gates several million dollars for his foundation, and I would like to invite you to Maine. I believe you would be the perfect person for my girls to train on how to start nonprofit agencies. Is this something you would be interested in doing?"

How could this amazing opportunity have simply dropped into my lap out of nowhere? I was ecstatic.

"She said they will train me how to start my nonprofit agency so I can build *Family Matters* into something huge. She used Bill Gates's name in the same sentence as mine, Darius! I can't believe this. I'm so excited. What do you think?" I asked.

He looked straight at me—his expression serious.

"No, you cannot go. You have to take care of the kids, Maria," he said, his tone resounding with finality.

"But Darius," I started.

"Maria," he answered, his expression stony. "You can't. End of story."

I was struggling to understand his negativity. This was such an incredible opportunity. It isn't every day that someone gets a call from Doris Buffet offering such a cool chance to grow something impactful.

Maybe he's right, I thought, considering everything I already had going on. That year alone, *Unity Bonds Initiative* and *Family Matters* partnered to host three Parent of the Year galas. A teatime for children raised fifteen thousand dollars for the Leukemia and Lymphoma Society. Plus, we produced *Heels on Broadway – Building Self Esteem,* which featured a mentoring event and fashion show. A week-long "Yes I Can! Summer Olympia," organized with the Little League, united dozens of families and disabled children with non-disabled partners for a week of sports and activities. I was very, very busy.

Everything was going so well, in fact, that Darius and I decided to take the whole family away for a week. The kids were now old enough to enjoy an adventure.

"What do you think about going to Magic Land?" I asked them over dinner one evening.

"No way. Really?" my son responded excitedly. "Yes!"

We packed our clothes and car and headed off for a total blast. It was so much fun!

"Again!" my daughter yelled after jumping off the steep waterslide and landing in the deep water with a splash. Her smile was bright, and her excitement was so infectious that we did it again!

Returning home feeling refreshed and happy didn't prepare me for what would come. Only a week later, I received a strange text from Darius.

Generally, it was his habit to come home directly after work. I was usually grilling chicken or some other summertime meal when he pulled in the driveway, but that night, I received a text message saying that "he was coming home to pack and leave."

"Where are we going?" I texted back, thinking he had some surprise planned and feeling a bit confused since we had just returned from vacation.

He didn't answer.

But when he came home, I was blown away by his words.

"I need a break—time for myself," he said.

Confused, I asked, "Time for yourself?"

Suddenly, I realized something as my mind flew back to the details of him leaving his previous wife. From what I understood, he had started acting odd (like he was doing now). It turned out he was tangled up with a woman from work. When his wife found out, she divorced him.

"Darius, I need you to be honest with me. Are you having an affair?" I asked.

He vehemently denied there was someone else.

"Don't be ridiculous, Maria. I told you already that I just need a break. Being away on vacation made me realize how stressed out I am. A little time away will be good for me," he explained.

At dinner, though, he told the children he was leaving. With little explanation, he packed his clothes, picked up our laptop, and walked out the front door.

And he didn't look back.

As Darius drove off, my kids clutched at me and cried. One was hanging onto my left leg and the other on my right, while the third was in my arms sobbing. The sound of them crying is etched on my brain—something I will never forget. They screamed so loud that the neighbor ran over, fearing someone had died.

"Oh, my gosh, Maria! Is everything okay?" she asked, out of breath from the run across the street.

"Darius just left us," I said in a stunned voice.

"What do you mean?" she asked, confusion running across her face.

"He came home, packed up his clothes, and said he needs time away from us," I answered.

"What?" she asked before saying, "Maria, I am so sorry."

The truth is that, in a way, I felt as though someone had died. In less than one hour, I had gone from being happily married, just home from a relaxing vacation, to becoming a separated mom of three. To make it all so much worse, I had no clue why.

In the following weeks, I was numb. I lost my appetite and dropped over ten pounds.

"Maria, are you okay? You are skin and bones," my colleague commented with concern.

I shrugged. I was emotionally drained and physically depleted. One night, my body started to hemorrhage. I called my family in Massachusetts, and they called 911. My son, already the little man, called his father.

"Daddy, Mommy is sick. You need to come home and take care of your family. It's your job as the man of the house!" he said. Such a brave little guy.

At the hospital, the staff asked if I was being abused. By then, Darius had joined me but was asked to leave the room when they started to question me.

"I think he's having an affair. He left us," I said, another bout of tears catching in my throat.

"Not good. Would you want to be tested for sexually transmitted diseases?" the doctor asked in a serious tone. I felt sick.

"Yes, I probably should," I answered.

Darius was incensed when he found out.

"So, this is how it's going to work," he said, his voice rising in anger. "I can't believe you said yes to the test. You are an embarrassment. Everyone in this hospital knows me." He stared at me, his hands trembling, before saying, "I'm taking the kids to the place I'm staying. You can call an Uber to take you home when they discharge you."

I cried even harder and went into a full-blown panic attack. He rolled his eyes, took the kids, and left.

The nurses on duty were sympathetic. "You are better off without him," one nurse said. "He shows up as such a family guy, but I see what he's really all about." She patted my hand and looked at me with such kindness that I felt a little better. "Cheer up, honey. You will be okay."

At 2:30 AM, I was discharged. I called an Uber, which dropped me off at the house. It was then I realized that I hadn't grabbed the house keys and had no way of getting in. I called Darius and then texted him when he didn't respond.

"You're being selfish. Figure it out," he replied.

I had no choice but to break a window and crawl into the house through the opening.

I called my mom when I woke up.

"Maria, I know this is hard. But you need to pull yourself together for the kids."

Our conversation brought me back to reality. I had never been one to give up, so despite my shock and disappointment, I needed to be strong for my kids. I would dig down to find the inner strength that I had always found before. None of us had asked to be left by the man we loved. We were in this together. Being the mom, I would figure it out. But I had no money, no real job, and although I was raising money for other organizations, I was making very little for our family. Plus, by then, I had realized that he had transferred money from our bank account and had left only one dollar in each of our joint accounts.

I called my neighbor, who was a close friend.

"My gut is telling me that there's another woman. I need to hire a private investigator," I said in a sorrowful voice. "I honestly don't believe Darius would leave because he needs time by himself."

"You may be right," she said. "But do you really want to know?"

"Yes, I do. Darius left us with nothing. I'm beginning to think this was all pre-planned. I found out last week that he cut off access to our bank accounts."

"What?!" she said, her expression aghast. "That's horrible!"

"Would you be willing to extend me a loan? You know I'm good for it," I said.

Less than a week later, the truth began to unfold when the investigator sent me pictures of Darius romancing a woman in a local restaurant. He had his fingers in her hair, and I noticed that he wasn't wearing his wedding band. A few days later, he was with another, sharing a glass of wine and kissing.

Days later, the investigator caught him spending a night with a former girlfriend at her house one town over. When the private investigator called, he asked to speak to my cousin.

"He thought it would be too painful for you to hear, Maria. He said that Darius has no morals," my cousin said as she pulled the investigator's report out of the printer and handed it to me.

I took the report, my hand shaking, and read it quickly.

Surveillance August 4, 2011

On this date, Ms. Maria Darius advised that she was out of town, and felt this would be a good opportunity to conduct surveillance on the subject. We commenced our surveillance at his workplace from the subject's work location.

At approximately 6:04 PM, we observed the subject depart the state police barracks wearing a suit. He departed alone in his Toyota, and we followed him. He ended up in the parking lot of the Jackson's restaurant. We observed Mr. Crowe enter the restaurant alone in a hurried manner. We noted the restaurant was extremely busy and after 5 minutes we entered.

Immediately after we entered, we noted Mr. Crowe standing in the entryway talking to an unknown female tall blonde in her late 20's-early 30's. We photographed both, Mr. Crowe and the unknown female. They gave off the impression they just recently met and were still getting to know each other while they laughed and giggled as they waited for their table.

After approx. 20 minutes, Mr. Crowe and his female friend sat at a small table, next to one another. They ordered a meal, and we observed the unknown female drinking wine. They sat close to each other and we could not hear their conversation as they talked, laughed, and giggled quietly amongst themselves. We returned outside and awaited his departure.

At 8:45 PM, we observed Mr. Crowe rush out of the restaurant alone, jump into his car and depart. We remained and observed the female Mr. Crowe was with, now sitting at the bar with a second unknown brunette female around the same age.

At 10:35 PM, both females depart the restaurant and the blonde departed in a Subaru Sedan. The brunette departed in a minivan. We followed the blonde in hopes she would again be meeting up *with the subject. We followed her to Keggers Bar and entered after talking on her cell phone for 5 minutes in her car.*

At 10:55 PM, we observed the subject arrive alone. He immediately entered the bar and took a seat at the bar next to the unknown blonde. They initially hugged, then spent the next 3 hours talking, laughing, and giggling while he drank martinis. We were successful in photographing them at the bar.

At approximately 1:30 AM, they departed together. The subject walked the unknown blonde to her car where they kissed briefly on the lips, hugged and departed in their separate vehicles. We were successful in videoing this interaction.

Once we determined the subject was heading home and the unknown blonde had gone the opposite way, we discontinued our surveillance at that time.

Surveillance August 5, 2011

We commenced our surveillance on this date at 8:15 PM, the subject departed and we followed him to Willowbrook Shopping Mall. We noted the subject was wearing plaid shorts and a blue shirt. We followed the subject on foot through the mall to a restaurant called Diana's Bistro. Once here, the subject meets up with a very young girl, whom we estimate to be approximately 20-21 years old. The subject and the girl get a table in the bar, and the subject buys them both a cocktail. They sit and talk quietly for over an hour and a half. At times, they can be seen laughing and giggling.

At 10:03 PM, the subject and the unknown female depart. They walk together toward the movie theatre, where the unknown female meets a group of her friends, all in their late teens-early 20s, and they get in line to buy movie tickets. The subject departs after giving the unknown girl a brief hug.

We then follow the subject to his marital residence. The subject is here for approximately half an hour and then departs. The subject does stop for gas and heads home, at which time we discontinue our surveillance.

Surveillance August 9, 2011

Once again, we commenced our surveillance on this date at the subject's place of employment at 7:30 PM. At 8:30 PM, the subject departed, and we followed him. The subject does stop for gas at a Mobil station and appears to be in quite a rush. We follow the subject who is driving at a high rate of speed to Wal-Mart. The subject parks, and walks very fast into Wal-Mart. We follow him inside and see him frantically searching the aisles. The subject ended up purchasing a greeting card, picture frame, and chocolates. The subject paid for his purchases and ran out the door.

We followed the subject, he parked in a driveway, and we noted the garage doors were shut. There were no other vehicles in the driveway. There were lights on in the kitchen and living room area. After about 25 minutes, we *observed the subject sitting at a table across from a blonde female, both drinking wine and heavily involved in conversation. This went on for well over 2 hours. We did photograph and video from our vantage from the street. We later identified the female in the pictures and video. Furthermore, we were able to determine that she was house-sitting for her aunt, who owns this residence and was currently out of town.*

After approximately 2 hours, we noted the house was dark and remained dark for an additional hour and a half before the subject departed. We discontinued our surveillance at that time.

Conclusions/Follow-up

We have determined that Darius Crowe is involved in meeting women on at least 3 occasions without his wife's knowledge, which appears to be from an online dating site and/or personal ad. In addition, we have observed this subject with an ex-girlfriend immediately after buying chocolates, a photo frame, and a greeting card from Walmart for an extended period of time in a dark house.

This was all done without his wife's knowledge, behind her back in a surreptitious way.

"He doesn't have any morals," I agreed, feeling my face flush with anger as I pictured Darius and a young girl. "Plus, he's so sure of himself that he's having his affairs right down the road from where his wife and kids live."

On several occasions, Darius called my cell phone to speak to the kids while the investigator, who had Darius in his sight, was sending pictures.

"Where are you?" I asked him one evening when the background noise sounded suspicious.

"I'm at the barracks in my office," he said. "I just wanted to talk to the kids. I'm working—I don't have time to talk to you."

The investigator's pictures told a different story. There he was cozied up to a pretty blonde at a local bar. I felt off-balance as my emotions flipped between heartbreak and anger. At that moment, I knew I could never trust him again.

"Cheaters rarely change their behavior," my brother said, his voice calm. "I think you know what you need to do."

My heart broke for both myself and my kids as I filed divorce paperwork several days later.

I decided to seek sole custody of our kids. I also filed for child support, an equitable distribution of marital assets, and spousal maintenance—I needed financial help.

Honestly, I was emotionally devastated and totally unprepared for the legal complexities of acquiring a divorce. Despite my experience in journalism, I had zero knowledge of the court system. I learned quickly that family law and local politics were waters I would need help navigating.

As a single mother with limited income, I focused on the kids and making ends meet. I imagined a regulated justice system with a speedy process following a linear set of laws. I was totally naïve and completely unprepared for the escalating level of acrimony and expensive legal disputes.

Bills piled up quickly, and I had no steady means of income. At that point, Darius was the primary breadwinner, a decision he convinced me was the most economical and best for our family.

We began negotiating informal agreements on child support, which were submitted to the court. Then Darius filed petitions to avoid his parental obligations, and I filed petitions to argue his. The back and forth of it all made me dizzy, almost like a glimpse into my not-too-distant future of playing ping pong in jail.

"He's NOT the person I thought he was," I told my brother one afternoon. "It's as though he's completely detached and is trying to hurt me for kicks. I don't understand. It's like he's possessed by something evil."

The Judge consistently favored Darius, frequently remarking about catching glimpses of him being interviewed on the news.

"I don't understand," I said to my lawyer. "Darius gets favored because he's known from his interviews on the news? What about the kids?"

During the divorce trial, Darius used legal tactics to delay court appearances. The more he stalled, the more time I went without court-ordered child support. I did everything I could to feed our kids but couldn't get a full-time job because I couldn't afford childcare. The process was financially bleeding me dry, which only increased the pressure.

I needed child support, and that became a central and consistent issue. During this time, Darius paid a mere three hundred dollars a month, or what equaled seventy-five dollars a week, toward supporting the kids. To make matters worse, he harassed and intimidated me outside of the courtroom.

"What are you doing here?" I asked one afternoon when I returned home to find him in the house. I had a court order that stated that he wasn't permitted to be there without my permission. He huffed out and jumped in his car, but I immediately noticed that my cell phone and a few other valuable items were suddenly missing.

I had no choice but to file an incident report with the State Police.

He had obviously been in the house again when I realized that my birth certificate, passport, and a 24-karat gold necklace worth over three thousand dollars, as well as the kids' passports and birth certificates, were missing. When I searched, I found that divorce-related paperwork, bank statements, a few pieces of furniture, and several other items were also gone.

Suddenly, I was feeling threatened.

"What if he becomes violent?" I asked my best friend. "This whole thing is scary. I don't know what to do."

"I know what I would do," she answered. "I would go to the police. I don't think you have a choice."

"I don't know if I should. It may make matters worse," I said.

In the end, I drove to the Willowbrook County Family Court and filed a petition seeking a judge's order of protection against Darius. Besides the missing items, the last few times he stopped at the house, when I tried to prevent him from coming in, he had put his foot in the door so that I couldn't close it. His aggressive reactions were making me nervous.

I felt relieved to see that the judge that day was female. Despite my pleas, though, she decided against the order of protection.

"Your honor, because you are refusing to do the right thing today, I really hope I don't have to come back here one day. It will be on you if anything happens to us," I said, keeping my tone respectful.

To make matters worse, she passed the request to the family court justice, Judge Greene, the same judge who was also serving as a Supreme Court justice and who had been assigned to our divorce case.

By then, I knew that Judge Greene had moved up through the powerful Willowbrook County political machine. He had served as a Willowbrook County attorney for thirteen years, at which point he won the election to the Family Court bench.

Eleven years later, Greene had moved into the role of the county's senior family court judge when another judge was forced to resign under the imminent threat of removal for violating the rights of four men who were sent to jail without legal representation or even a hearing.

A month or so later, I found myself in front of Judge Greene once again to seek an order of protection. It turned out to be a brief and shocking experience.

After informing me of my rights, Judge Greene asked me if I had filed and signed the petition on my own.

"On my own?" I asked, needing clarification of his question.

"Without an attorney," he answered.

"Yes, your honor," I responded.

That was all he asked before dismissing the petition on a technicality.

"It does not appear to state a cause of action under Article 8 of the Family Court Act. No release is, of course, granted."

I watched in disbelief as he flung my petition for the order of protection behind his back, where it hit the floor with a resounding "slap."

Unfortunately, Judge Greene's dismissal of the order of protection only further emboldened Darius. As we contested the terms of our divorce in court, he continued harassing me.

I found notes and other evidence of his presence inside my parked vehicle in various places. I was so unnerved that I reported many of the incidents to the

State Police, hoping they would intervene. But since he worked with them, nothing was done.

During divorce depositions, Darius shockingly presented an audio recording of me practicing stress-relief exercises and positive affirmations. As a way to release the high levels of stress I was under, I repeated, "I have more than enough money. I have plenty of money to pay my bills."

I recorded one session and practiced sitting with my eyes closed, listening to it several times a day. That recording was saved only on my computer at home. Hearing it in the courtroom was alarming.

"Where did you get that?" I asked, knowing it had been stored on my desktop and nowhere else.

"I found it on my iPad," he responded, his expression innocuous. His angle was to present the recording as evidence that I had money.

"Judge, you hear for yourself her saying on this recording that she has more than enough money," he said.

Darius started texting me, saying, "Maria, you are using this word too much with your attorney." Or "You keep misspelling your attorney's name."

The whole thing was driving me nuts. How did he know what I was doing? I thought he was just playing with me.

Suddenly, I grew cold. Had Darius somehow hacked into my computer? How else could he know what I was doing on my computer in the house?

"You need to report this to the FBI," my colleague said, his tone serious.

"The FBI?" I asked, incredulous.

However, the next day, when I received a message from Darius commenting on an email he would have only seen on my computer, I felt I had no other choice.

After hearing my story, the FBI agent said, "I suggest you hire an IT expert. It's the best way to find evidence of an unlawful break into your computer. If a break is confirmed, then you will need to take it to the State Police."

"But he works for the State Police," I said, feeling exasperated.

"Do what you need to do," he said.

I hired a computer and networking consultant within twenty-four hours, and within thirty minutes of looking at my computer, he confirmed an installed keylogger.

"What is a keylogger?" I asked, both hopeful and nervous. If Darius had broken into my computer, I would have evidence that he had all my information, and my entire case would have been compromised.

"A keylogger is a covert software that can be used to record keyboard strokes, monitor the actions of anyone using the computer, and obtain information, such as passwords," he answered.

The consultant printed a copy of the evidence and handed it to me.

"Good luck, ma'am," he said as he left.

The next day, I made the short trip to the State Police Barracks with my computer and the documentation from the IT specialist praying I wouldn't run into Darius.

"He has information that he could have only gotten off my personal computer. The IT expert I hired told me that if I had been hacked, I would be able to track who did it," I told the investigator.

"You're in luck," the officer said with a smile. "We have the best team for handling these types of issues."

Four months went by without a word from them.

Finally, I contacted the Troopers to find out what had been taking so long. They, in turn, directed me to Judge Greene.

My frustrations were building as I spoke with Judge Greene. He ignored my findings and said, "Mrs. Crowe, enough of these ridiculous accusations." Then he smiled at Darius and said, "Mr. Crowe, I saw you give that interview on the McKenna case yesterday. Great job."

Darius countered my filing for an order of protection by filing one against me.

"She's been hacking my computer," he told the judge. The judge admonished me but dismissed Darius's petition.

When the State Police finally got back to me, I received disappointing news.

"There's nothing we can do. We couldn't trace the IP address to the keylogger. Half of the evidence had been deleted from the computer," the State Police investigator said.

"But you told me you had him. What do you mean there's nothing you can do?" I asked, doing my best to keep the frustration out of my voice.

"Talk to Judge Greene about it," he said.

Oh, please, I'm not that naïve, I thought.

Things continued to get worse. Despite a court-ordered freeze on our assets due to the divorce filing, Darius removed my name from a life insurance policy and cashed out its six-thousand-dollar value for himself. I didn't know anything about it until I received an email from a company employee confirming that the insurance had been canceled. At the same time, I learned he had also cashed out a CD worth thirty thousand dollars that was an inheritance from my parents.

The stress mounted when Darius failed to make the car insurance payments. Randomly, a State Police officer pulled me over and asked to see my insurance card.

"I could take your car right now," he said when he checked the insurance and shared that it was out of date. I started crying.

"My ex-husband is responsible for keeping the insurance paid up," I said. "Does this mean he's not doing that?"

With the car insurance company threatening to cancel, I had to call my attorney.

"He's moving money into accounts that I didn't know existed. Please, can you help me? I need car insurance," I pleaded. "He's violating the agreements. You need to make him accountable."

"I'll take care of it," she assured me.

With credit card debt accumulated from Darius's prior marriage and costs that he promised to pay but wasn't handling, I felt as though I was literally crumbling under the burden.

The judge would not grant my subpoena request to obtain the old credit card bills, which would prove they were not debts from our marriage. At the time of our separation, we had paid off his college loans, but my college debt remained open and due.

"For the whole ten years we were married, Darius insisted on handling the money and paying the bills. I trusted him. Every check I received was deposited directly into our accounts, and he paid the bills. But he never paid my college loan," I told my brother. Shaking my head in disbelief, I said, "This just can't be real."

"What a mess," my brother agreed.

I'm sure by this point, you're thinking it can't get any worse. Well, it did. Darius transferred hundreds of dollars in debt he owed to the water authority into my name without my knowledge. I learned about the move when I received a letter from a collection agency. Quickly, the water was canceled for nonpayment. I returned home one night to find a fluorescent sheet of paper taped to the front door and a hole dug in the front yard.

I went to the neighbor's house to ask if they had seen what happened.

"Maria, it was the water department. They came and turned off your water today. That's why the hole is there."

"What?!?" I asked. "They are leaving us with no water?"

Only two days later, the power was shut off on the hottest day of the year.

In the separation of assets, the judge awarded Darius our Toyota Sienna, the car I purchased after Darius insisted I sell my beautiful white Mercedes in favor of a minivan, and I was left with the rusty, older family minivan that had died months earlier.

"This is all so wrong," I said, tears of anger and frustration pouring down my face. "What kind of person leaves the mother of his children with no way to get around?"

Finally, after more than two years of bitter fighting both in and out of the courtroom, the judge released an official judgment of divorce and set orders regarding child custody, access, and support.

To celebrate my freedom, I literally hit downtown Willowbrook to skip through the streets.

"I'm free! I'm finally free!" I laughed, feeling happy for the first time in over two years.

Judge Greene ordered Darius and I to share equal physical and legal custody of the kids. His order included setting custodial conditions and times on a rotating schedule.

"I want a fixed schedule," Darius demanded. "I have a life, and I stick to an agenda."

"Sure, he does," I said to my attorney. "He wants to be sure the schedule is convenient for him and his girlfriend."

Since it was Darius who abandoned the premises, I was awarded exclusive use of the home.

"You are ordered to work together to prepare the house to be sold," Judge Greene dictated.

However, he provided no equitable distribution of our assets, nor did he declare a ruling for higher education costs for the kids. To add to the stress, the child support order was made in Darius's favor.

Child support is calculated using a specific formula based on the Child Support Stands Act (CSSA). First, there is parental income where both parents' gross incomes are combined. A percentage of the combined income is used depending on how many children need support.

One child: 17%

Two children: 25%

Three children: 29%

Four children: 31%

Five+ children: 35% or more.

There are other factors that come into play such as health insurance, child care costs, educational needs and extraordinary expenses.

You may not know that child support is mandatory in any divorce involving minor children in New York. It's intended to help cover food, shelter, and clothing expenses, and I learned that it is usually based on the parents' incomes and how many children need to be covered. According to the state mandate, three children would account for twenty-nine percent of Darius's income. The determination would be made by examining his most recent federal income tax return.

Plus, it can take into consideration past employment and future earning capacity.

"Why is the judge blowing off the state mandate?" I asked my attorney when Darius was ordered to pay seven hundred fifty-five dollars a month in support. "He's making a hundred thirty thousand."

My projects were barely paying for themselves, but the judge estimated my salary at thirty thousand. At the time, any money I made went directly back into the show.

Without explaining his decision, Judge Greene provided no stipulation for retroactive child support costs. Plus, I was not granted spousal support despite the law stating I was entitled based on Darius's leaving the marriage. That payment would have been thirty-two hundred dollars per month, but I received nothing. Beyond that, Darius was not ordered to return the money he had stolen from my inheritance or to pay an equal part of my student loan debt as we had paid his while we were together.

One of the judge's biggest oversights was failing to require Darius to send child support payments through the Child Support Enforcement Unit. The enforcement unit has powers outside the courts to enforce payments, such as suspending driver's licenses for unpaid support.

Working outside the collections unit made it nearly impossible to hold Darius accountable. Instead of having the amount deducted from his bank account on the first of each month, I often had to humiliate myself by begging him to fulfill his obligation.

And then, believe it or not, things got worse.

Chapter Five

INJUSTICE

"Life is not about waiting for the storms to pass but learning to dance in the rain."

~Vivian Greene

The following two years after our divorce officially turned out to be the most tumultuous and transformative years of my life.

Somehow, I managed to keep our home together for the sake of the kids, but honestly, I spent most of my days living in a haze of disbelief.

I distracted myself by expanding the *Family Matters* brand on a website called *FamilyMattersWithMaria.com*. I was also hired as the main on-air personality for Viewpoint Media Network, an independent television station focused on our region's community affairs. In that position, I became the face of a 30-minute show called *EmPowerHer*.

Soon afterward, a *Family Matters* sponsor unexpectedly nominated me for National American Miss, a nationwide pageant designed to empower women and foster community service.

American Miss wasn't about winning a crown—it was about gaining a voice to raise awareness about important topics of the time. Judging was based on personal conduct and a record of making a difference through community services.

The competition was so much fun. I could barely believe it when I won the state title and was to be sent on to the national competition. There, I met other incredible women doing amazing work, and I knew the judges had a difficult choice to make. When the winner was to be called, I held my breath.

"Second place goes to...Maria Crowe!"

The following year, once again, a *Family Matters* sponsor nominated me for National Miss. This time, my platform was *Empowering Voices Against Domestic Violence.*

For the second year in a row, I was awarded first place.

"Congratulations, Maria! You will now go on to represent New York State in the national competition!"

Six serious-faced judges grilled me on my experiences.

"Tell me more about that, Mrs. Crowe. How were you able to create and launch your show all by yourself?"

"It wasn't easy. I wanted to create something that would make a difference to families, but I was also committed to my own family. Sometimes, I had to make tough choices," I explained.

"Examples, please," said one gray-haired, confidence-exuding judge.

Smiling, I answered every question with confidence. I was proud of my accomplishments and enjoyed sharing what I was doing. Once more, I knew the judges didn't have an easy choice in picking a winner.

"And the winner is..."

We waited expectantly, each holding our breath. I was overwhelmed with excitement and gratitude when I heard my name echo through the sound system.

"Thank you!" I cried excitedly as I stepped forward to accept a crown and a beautiful trophy.

When the local paper declared me one of Willowbrook's Most Influential Women for Community Service, I was overcome by emotion.

"This is amazing," I told my kids the day of the announcement. "When you believe in something, and you work hard to bring your dream to fruition, you can accomplish anything you desire."

During my acceptance speech, I said, "Winning this award is one of the greatest honors of my life. I do the work not to win awards but to help families grow and thrive. This award is just an added bonus." I will admit that I was thrilled to wear the crown and hold the trophy they handed me.

My dream of creating something impactful was coming together even as I was still dealing with the ramifications of my divorce from Darius.

When Judge Greene declared Darius and I divorced, he was clear on one issue.

"You two will need to resolve your outstanding disputes regarding property and assets," he said, his tone stern and his expression somber.

Judge Greene then signed an order giving me exclusive rights to the home.

When I asked about the repairs, he said, "That includes anything that needs to be done to repair the home." Then he added, "Mr. Crowe should not enter the home without the express permission of Mrs. Crowe."

The priority in my mind was fixing the house to make it saleable.

"Darius, we need to get this done," I said repeatedly. However, completing the repairs required cooperation, and Darius inevitably made excuses or delayed paying for his share of the projects, which prevented the necessary progress.

While the house required some basic work when we moved in eleven years earlier, it gradually fell into disrepair. A pipe leaked right before Darius left us, damaging the interior.

"I called a restoration company, and they're coming to do an estimate today," I told him.

When the insurance check arrived shortly afterward, Darius called to say he had deposited it, which was okay with me. We had agreed that either one of us could endorse any insurance checks without the signature of the other. Doing so would speed up the process of getting the damage repaired.

But a short while after the original damage occurred, a massive storm blew through our area, causing even more damage.

"This is fucking unbelievable," I said as I surveyed the storm damage caused by torrential rain coupled with horrific winds. The siding was torn off the side of the house, and the pool area was damaged.

Once more, I filed a claim to cover the damages. This time, the estimate was just under three thousand dollars.

"We'll need to come up with a thousand dollars to cover the deductible," I told Darius.

"Oh, we will?" he answered, his tone snide.

I swallowed my frustration, slid the insurance check inn the amount of one thousand thirteen dollars and twenty cents into my purse, and headed to the bank, where there appeared to be an event going on. My three kids and a former student who accompanied us that day stopped to investigate the celebration while I walked to the teller window, smiling at the young woman there.

"It looks like something fun is going on," I said as I endorsed the check with my initials, as was my habit. I passed the check through the window, and the teller pointed to my initials.

"Is this your signature?" she asked, her blue eyes meeting mine.

"Yes," I answered. The bank vice president, who was chatting with another employee, looked over the teller's shoulder.

With a quick smile in my direction, she said, "You should print your name below your initials."

The teller slid the check back to me.

"Sure," I responded with an answering smile, simultaneously wondering what the purpose was. It seemed apparent that I was the only person who had signed the check. But I did what she asked and passed it back to the teller.

With the deposit made and cleared, I hired a contractor to repair the siding and pool and covered the one-thousand-dollar deductible myself.

The old me, the person who had not yet been baptized into the underbelly of an unfair system, was naïve enough to think that would be the end of the matter. However, with the experience I gained through what happened next, I learned differently.

We are talking about Darius here: a man who first committed adultery, second lied about it, third deserted his family, and fourth defaulted on his liabilities to his kids. If I had thought about it from that perspective at the time, I would have thought differently.

Financial pressures were mounting, and I was feeling the stress. I was earning considerably less than in the past and now was saddled with ridiculous legal bills. The house required constant upkeep, and the incidental costs related to raising our kids, who lived with me the lion's share of the time, were also piling up. The situation had become dire.

"I think I'm going to have to sell my jewelry," I admitted to my brother.

"Don't do that," he said. "You can come up with a better way."

But I couldn't. I had so much responsibility that I couldn't take on another job. At four, six, and seven years old, my kids needed me. At the same time, though, the situation had gotten to the point that, as I stood at the podium accepting an award one evening, I worried there would be no electricity in the house when I got home. I was making payments, but I will admit that I was several months behind.

"You can't saddle me with all of this, Darius. What is the matter with you? These are your children."

He laughed, his tone scornful.

When I realized that a set of high-end golf clubs I had purchased for him weeks before he abandoned us was missing, I became suspicious that he had been in the house.

"Darius, what happened to the golf clubs? Did you take them? I was looking for them to sell, but I can't find them. I need to either return them or sell them to pay the credit card I purchased them on," I said.

He laughed again and then hung up on me.

The Judge had ordered Darius, who was earning an annual salary of nearly one hundred thirty-five thousand dollars, to pay only seven hundred fifty-five dollars a month in support of our three kids. Still, he often held that payment over us and constantly ignored portions of property repair costs and the kids' dental care.

The proverbial shit hit the fan when a faulty pipe in the house busted completely, flooding the kitchen and part of the basement.

"This CAN'T be happening," I said as I surveyed the damage.

Once more, I called the restoration company, which took care of the immediate damage. The entire kitchen was gutted and then dried with sand, and several windows, walls, and pipes were replaced.

The insurance company estimated the repairs at twenty-five thousand seven hundred seventy-eight dollars. A check was issued that was intended to fix the kitchen, windows, interior and exterior walls, and plumbing.

Behind the scenes and without my knowledge, though, Darius jockeyed to gain control over the payment. I learned later that he called the insurance company and asked a representative if they would send correspondence to a different address. Thankfully, his request was denied.

I also later learned that the company had declined his request to remove my name from another check and reissue it, making it payable only to him.

"I never wanted this situation to become so bitter," I told my mom one late afternoon. "This is all so horrible. It's so wrong—all of it," I said tearfully.

Under these exceedingly difficult circumstances, I felt forced to reexamine the terms of the divorce judgment, especially the level of child support that the judge assigned us. In the original order, I was awarded much less than the amount entitled by law. I needed help.

Then, one evening, I received a call from Darius.

"Hi, Maria," he said, his voice chipper and friendly.

Immediately, something felt off, and I became suspicious. Why was he being so nice? It had been nearly three years since he had been even the least bit friendly.

"What's up," I asked, doing my best to match his chipper tone.

"Maria, I just wanted to call to find out how many checks you cashed from the insurance," he said.

That's weird, I thought. He just used my name twice. I wonder what he's up to?

"The insurance company says the policy is canceled. I just need to know how many checks have been issued."

He started listing check amounts one by one, each time hesitating and waiting for me to confirm.

Suddenly, a cold shiver ran down my spine.

Oh, my God, I think he's recording this conversation, I thought.

"Darius, I think you need to call my attorney," I said, the calm tone of my voice hiding the sudden anxiety that was making my heart race.

After he hung up, I quickly dialed the insurance company. The representative confirmed that Darius had asked to remove my name from the plan and to change the mailing address on our account to that of his girlfriend.

Thankfully, the insurance company denied his request, and our account was now flagged.

Not long afterward, I received a message from a State Police Investigator who worked in Darius's barracks asking me to give him a call. I dialed immediately.

"This is Maria Crowe returning the call of Investigator Murphy," I said.

The investigator and I spoke for nearly half an hour. During the conversation, I sensed that he was fishing for information about the check I had signed and deposited at the bank on the day of the community event three years earlier while Darius and I were still married.

"Have I broken any laws?" I asked.

To my relief, he replied, "No, ma'am, you haven't."

"Okay, good," I said. "I deposited the check, and the money was used for the intended repairs," I explained.

Things got weirder after that conversation. The State Police began to call my divorce attorney repeatedly. In an affidavit filed later, my attorney recalled how the investigator advised her that Darius was urging the State Police officer to arrest me for signing the one thousand thirteen dollar and twenty cent check. My attorney reiterated to the investigator that I was attempting to resolve several issues related to the divorce and our marital property.

Still, the investigator accused me of cashing the check without Darius's signature. We produced a copy of another insurance check for a much larger amount that Darius had cashed without my signature. The investigator switched gears and asked if I had a private bank account. This concerned my lawyer.

"Maria, if I were you, I would hire a good criminal lawyer. I have a bad feeling about this," she said, a worried look in her eyes.

Feeling furious, I said, "Where is the justice in this fucking system? I should have equal treatment. Why is it that each time I complain to the State Police, it falls on deaf ears, but they never investigated Darius even when I had proof that he hacked my fucking computer! Plus, we showed them that he signed a check without me. How is that any different than me signing a check without him?"

As my attorney advised, I drove to the State Police barracks praying the whole way not to bump into Darius to talk to the investigator about the fact that Darius was using my name and social security number to obtain credit cards and other financial benefits. The investigator gave me an odd look.

"I'll be right back," he said, looking over his shoulder at me before disappearing into the back room.

When he returned some twenty minutes later, he said, "Maria, you will need to come back with your attorney to file the complaint. However, I do have a question about a certain insurance check."

"Okay, let's get this straight," I said, looking him straight in the eye. "So, you're telling me that I need to bring my attorney to file a complaint, but I don't need her with me to discuss an issue with a check?" I stepped back for a minute, studying him. His actions suddenly felt very suspect.

"Are you working for my ex-husband?" I asked.

He said nothing, so in disgust, I grabbed my papers and stamped toward the door, angrily pulling it open.

"That's the bathroom," the investigator said.

"Yes, I can see that," I said before stomping out the front door.

I later learned that the investigator had recorded my entire visit that day without saying a word. Suddenly, I no longer trusted the State Police to investigate allegations with any kind of impartiality.

"I need to file a formal complaint with the State Police Internal Affairs," I told my attorney. "I can't just let this go. It's not right."

The complaint included questioning why nothing had been done about my computer being hacked, my stolen passport, items missing from my mailbox, and the general harassment that had become a challenging part of my life since the divorce.

I received a response from a New York State Police Deputy Superintendent three days later.

"Be assured that a thorough review will be made into this matter," the commander wrote.

I am a smart woman, so I had a good sense that going over the local police's head probably wasn't the best way to win with law enforcement, but I honestly felt I had no choice. I had reached my limit.

Once more, I heard nothing.

It was then that I realized I needed to find an ally. Darius was demanding the police arrest me for signing and depositing the check, and since he worked there, he had their ear.

So, I was forced to make a huge decision—one I suspected would have resounding repercussions.

That autumn, I commenced a petition to claim unpaid child support and outstanding orthodontic bills. I also sought an appropriate increase in child support and retroactive support payments. I argued that the law provided for an increase on the grounds that Darius was making a lot more money than he had been and that he was not fulfilling his current child support obligations.

Although I knew Darius would resent this action, I honestly never imagined he would stoop so low as to lobby co-workers and prosecutors to have the mother of his children arrested for doing the same thing he had done—depositing insurance checks with one signature.

Judge Greene signed an order late that fall in which he decided some of the concerns outlined in my petitions.

First, he ordered that we (Darius and I) list and sell the residence together, and second, that profits be split fifty-fifty.

Judge Greene also set parental schedules for holidays, school breaks, and birthdays.

Once again, though, the child support issue went unaddressed.

As if that wasn't enough, in an outrageous move that came out of nowhere, Judge Greene ordered me to sign and turn over the twenty-five-thousand-dollar insurance check to Darius, who, in the words of the judge, "shall determine how the proceeds from the insurance check shall be used to improve the residence."

This directive reversed a previous court decision that assigned me the exclusive right to direct and manage home upgrades.

"This is insane," I ranted. "Why would Judge Greene do something like this? At this rate, this house will never get fixed. This is infuriating."

Shortly after that, Judge Greene suddenly and without explanation recused himself from the case, which set off a chain of additional recusals.

Less than two weeks later, the Supreme Court Justice who had been the first woman elected to the Supreme Court in New York's Fourth Judicial District recused herself from judging the case, citing "a potential conflict." That recusal was followed by yet another a week later, once again, with no explanation.

The stage was now set.

Chapter Six

PERSECUTION

"Justice will not be served until those who are unaffected are as outraged as those who are."

~Benjamin Franklin

The levee broke right after the first of the year when I received a call from the State Police.

"Mrs. Crowe, you need to turn yourself in at the Meadow Park State Police Barracks," the officer instructed.

Just after 2:30 p.m. on the day before my son's birthday, I was arrested on charges of second-degree forgery, a felony, and petty larceny.

"Stand right there," the officer instructed before snapping a photo that would be my mug shot. Next, I was escorted to where I would be fingerprinted. My mind was struggling to believe what was happening as each finger was rolled over the ink pad and pressed onto the paper in front of me. Thumb. Index finger. Middle finger. Ring finger. Pinky finger. The same process was repeated on my left hand.

I recognized the trooper taking my fingerprints from my daughter's school. The anxiety I was feeling prompted a little sauciness, so I said, "Your job must be difficult when you're booking someone who is actually guilty."

He glanced at me for just a moment and then back to the job at hand.

I felt as if I were watching someone else having their fingers rolled in black ink. It all felt so unreal.

Why is Darius trying to destroy me? I thought. What did I ever do to him but love him?

I later obtained a written statement from the State Police reporting that Darius specifically asked troopers to investigate and arrest me for depositing the check for one thousand thirteen dollars and twenty cents that he had been badgering me about. Both Darius and the same investigator who told me I needed my attorney present to file a complaint (but who was fine with asking me about the check without one present) signed the statement.

I was stunned that it had come down to this. How could a man stoop so low that he would have the mother of his children arrested on a trumped-up charge? He cheated on me, he left our family, and now he was trying to destroy me and destroy our kids by default. The whole thing felt insane.

For a moment, though, I felt hopeful. This could be my opportunity to tell my side of the story. So, I grabbed my purse and headed over to the police barracks. At the time, I was still naïve enough to believe that once I had the chance to explain the facts of what happened, I would be released and allowed to go on with my life.

The whole arrest procedure felt bizarre. The station was practically empty, and I wasn't handcuffed. I was left to sit on a bench with my attorney, staring at the clock on the wall that was ticking off the seconds. With each passing minute, I felt my anger and disbelief growing. I needed to do something, so I prayed.

"God, please, I need a sign that you are here and you're listening," I whispered.

The answer came immediately.

"The computers just crashed," the booking officer announced.

I laughed and muttered to myself, "Maria, it's okay. You're going to be okay."

My attorney turned to me with a warning expression. He put two fingers to his lips, signaling me to stop talking. When the computers powered back up a full thirty minutes later, the questioning began.

"What's your job description," the trooper asked, his tone flavored with a hint of sarcasm.

"Reporter," I answered.

"Hmm, I don't have that here. I'll record it as miscellaneous." He must have found that funny because he chuckled.

As the questioning continued, only a few miles away, Darius was picking my kids up from school. I can't imagine the glee he must have been feeling when he told them, "Mom was arrested. She did something bad."

I knew that was coming.

"We should hold a press conference so that I can tell my side of the story. My ex is trying to destroy me. I have a feeling he will try to blast me in the media," I told my attorney.

"Your arrest wouldn't make headlines, Maria. It's not newsworthy. Holding a press conference wouldn't make sense. Let's face it—we're talking about a bad divorce and a marital check," he said.

"I think you're wrong," I said. "Darius is a narcissist who works for the the State Police, and he's trying to destroy my reputation for God knows what reason. Plus, he thinks this is all funny. I honestly think we need to do something."

"Seriously, Maria. You're being overdramatic. You're good. Don't worry about it." His tone had a note of finality, so I let it go. But I should have trusted my gut.

The press release the State Police issued, which was more than likely written by Darius, made it sound like I had defrauded a bank. Darius grasped the opportunity to make me look bad. He contacted multiple media outlets; my arrest made the evening news on numerous channels, reaching approximately half a million households.

My arraignment was held in front of Town Justice Benjamin Hughes on the same day. It was then that I learned I was facing a criminal trial and two and a third to seven years in jail. I couldn't believe it.

The collateral damage of my arrest was heartstopping.

In a matter of hours, everything that I had spent years building fell apart. View Point Media Network and Channel 11 dropped me like a hot potato, and Family Matters, my pet project for years, came to a screeching halt.

I also lost four New York State marketing contracts worth sixty thousand dollars.

I later learned that Darius had contacted National Miss, emailing them my mug shot, hoping they would strip me of one of my proudest achievements.

Being portrayed as a criminal through the media made it almost impossible to find a job. I needed health benefits and food and clothing for the kids. But between the arrest and the subsequent media coverage, which was portraying me as a criminal, I was struggling to get anyone to even speak with me. Not only did I have no income, but I also couldn't even collect unemployment.

With barely a cent to my name, I needed to find a way to hire a criminal defense attorney.

In the beginning years of the fiasco that had become my life, I still trusted the system. That trust cost me and the kids an enormous amount of time, money, and pain. I was careful when it came to finding someone to handle this case.

After researching, I hired a reasonably outspoken Willowbrook Democrat who practiced family and criminal law.

"I think this guy is exactly the kind of attorney I need," I confided to a friend. He has a great reputation and is also active politically. Being politically connected seems to be important in this county."

"Why do you say that?" my friend asked, a quizzical expression on her face.

"Experience," I answered.

My experience was hard-earned. Two years after hiring a divorce attorney on the advice of a colleague, the case was still ongoing and unresolved. Why was I losing nearly every time I stood in front of a judge? Some petitions were denied without hearings, and my attorney had missed an important appeal deadline.

After the arrest, my attorney sent a letter to Darius's attorney.

"Please instruct your client to have no further direct contact with my client by any means, including texts, emails, phone calls, or face-to-face conversations. He is simply not a safe person for my client to have any contact with while the criminal charges are pending. This is an unnecessary complication, but we will have to do our best to deal with it," it said.

He then conducted an extensive investigation into the passing of the check. Shortly afterward, we formally requested to dismiss the case to the Willowbrook County Assistant District Attorney (ADA) Deidre Kendall, who was assigned to prosecute it.

A copy of the one thousand thirteen dollar and twenty cent check was enclosed, showing that I had signed it twice—once using my initials followed by a legible signature, just as the bank vice president suggested the day the deposit was made. The initials matched previous deposits and in no way resembled Darius's signature.

We also produced other checks showing how I generally signed my name. Each one matched the signature of the "felonious" check.

"This is not a felony forgery case," my attorney wrote. "Arguably, the bank should not have cashed it or even allowed her to deposit the check without both spouses' signatures. The fact that they did does not make Maria guilty of possessing a forged instrument. Nothing is forged about this check...her initials are not a forgery of her ex-husband's name. I ask you to review this with whatever handwriting expert you need."

"Thank you," I said when he shared the letter before sending it. "I don't think it can be any clearer that this is all a farce."

The letter was sent, but no response was received, so my attorney contacted the ADA again in May.

(Keep in mind as you read this that each time my attorney had to contact me again, I was billed for his time.)

This time, his letter said, "I have repeatedly explained that Mr. Crowe also cashed checks that were made out to both Mr. and Mrs. Crowe. Prosecution should cease immediately."

Once again, no response was received, forcing us to request a preliminary hearing.

"All defendants accused of committing felony crimes are entitled to preliminary hearings. Those hearings are supposed to be held within days of the arrest," he wrote.

For some reason, the Willowbrook DA refused to participate in a preliminary hearing, so the Meadow Park Court scheduled it instead.

"Incarceration is not a prerequisite to a preliminary hearing," my attorney argued. "And, as of this date, the defense accepts no further speedy trial delay." In other words, it was time to get proceedings moving.

A dismissal was argued on several grounds.

First, the evidence prosecutors produced was insufficient to support the second-degree criminal possession of a forged instrument charge, as stated in the grand jury's indictment.

"Under state penal law, Mrs. Crowe is not guilty of felony forgery because she did not forge a signature, nor did she intend harm, fraud, or deception. To charge criminal possession of a forged instrument, the prosecutor must show that there was specific intent to defraud, deceive, or injure Mr. Crowe," he argued.

"I didn't use the money from the insurance check to buy clothes or go on a fancy vacation," I said in frustration as we prepared my defense. "It went to fix the damned house. And if you want to get technical, only Darius benefitted from the repairs when we sold the place," I added with a sniff. "Does that count at all?"

In the courtroom, my attorney handed over paperwork to the judge. "Here is a copy of the insurance check for two thousand seven hundred twenty five dollars that Mr. Crowe signed *without* including the signature of his ex-wife, Maria Crowe."

If there is any fairness at all in our legal system, dismissal should have occurred in the interest of justice.

The prosecutor's next statement was so outrageous that I thought my head would explode.

"Judge, we are not pursuing criminal charges against Mr. Crowe because we do not want to spend any more valuable time or money on this case."

"What the hell?" I whispered to my attorney. Anger bolted through me, starting in my head and traveling like lightning through my entire body. "By charging me and not Darius, these people are engaging in selective prosecution, aren't they? Why is there a double standard?"

"There seems to be," he said sternly before turning his attention back to the proceedings.

On the way out of the courthouse, I was feeling even angrier.

"I think any sane person would recognize the fact that the DA's Office should have disqualified itself from prosecuting the case on that basis alone. What is the matter with these people?" I was incensed.

"Look, Maria, I guarantee you that he doesn't have a case," he said. "We'll win, and when we do, we'll sue the county and the State Police for false arrest."

The anger I had been working so hard to hold back dissipated a bit.

"You're sure," I said rather than asking. He nodded.

"I'm sure," he said.

"Okay. This is all so wrong. It's infuriating," I said, biting back my anger. "If I committed a crime, so did Darius."

I wanted to stamp my feet and scream at the injustice, but my attorney continued to ask me to be patient. I had been patient up to now, very patient, in fact, but my patience was running thin.

Then, believe it or not, things got even crazier.

The DA presented my case to a grand jury, this time changing the charge against me. The second-degree forgery charge was dropped, and the grand jury indicted me on criminal possession of a forged instrument, a second-degree felony, and petit larceny.

We weren't provided with the transcripts of the grand jury proceedings, so we had to believe that the indictment was secured without sufficient evidence.

And the injustices continued.

By failing to respond to my attorney's requests for discovery, which is the information on witnesses and evidence that would be presented at trial, the prosecutors violated New York's Criminal Procedure Law.

The delay prevented us from adequately preparing for trial and was just one more example of why the charge should have been thrown out.

My attorney suggested we file a motion seeking sanction for failing to comply with the law.

"What does that mean?" I asked, even though I was pretty sure I knew. I was becoming savvier with experience.

"It means that the case can be thrown out because they didn't follow through on their responsibility," he answered.

The DA's Office finally responded by sending some of the overdue discovery material later that year.

The delay in obtaining the material severely hampered our defense, putting us at a big disadvantage in preparing motions.

To make matters more complicated, the DA's Office continued to clash with my attorney, a candid Democrat who had challenged Judge Greene, a Republican, for Family Court Judge several years before.

"I think I'm going to need to hire a new lawyer," I said to my brother over dinner. "This is all sick enough without having politics involved."

"Why do you think it's political?" he asked, his expression curious.

"What else could it be?" I answered. "It's become pretty clear to me that there is bad blood between my lawyer and the judge. Their egos are costing me money. I have to put an end to this."

I hired a new criminal defense attorney who was reputed to have a better working relationship with the ADA prosecuting the case.

In the meantime, the lawyer bills were piling up.

One night, after the kids had gone to bed, my mom called.

"How are you, honey?" she asked, trying unsuccessfully to mask her concern with a chipper tone.

"I'm okay, Mom," I answered, even though I wasn't. I was in the middle of adding the latest lawyer bills to a spreadsheet, and the new total was almost eighty thousand dollars.

My new criminal defense attorney came recommended by a friend, which made me feel a bit more confident that he knew what he was doing. He explained the risks of going to trial, but he also guaranteed we would win.

'Maria, the DA, and your ex have no case. It's clear that this is a divorce case and nothing more."

"You're sure," I said, once more making a statement rather than asking.

"You have a very good case, Maria. When this piece is over, I will help you pursue your ex-husband for malicious arrest," he said.

"We can do that?" I asked.

"Absolutely," he answered with a confident grin.

"That would be wonderful," I said, a relieved smile relaxing my face.

For the first time in a long while, I felt hopeful. Things were finally looking up.

"The DA has offered us an adjournment in contemplation of dismissal," my new attorney said.

"What does that mean?" I asked, by now knowing from experience that I needed to get absolute clarity on everything.

"It simply means that your case would be adjourned and ultimately dismissed if you plead guilty to a misdemeanor and stay arrest-free," he explained. "I don't have a crystal ball, Maria, so nothing is a guarantee, but I believe in you and the case, and I like to win."

"I like the sound of winning," I said, his confidence building my own. "But I have to be honest. I don't like the idea of pleading guilty."

I had been jerked around enough by the system, and by now, I knew I didn't want to play their games.

"Look, Maria, it's the first time that I have someone sitting in that chair who is innocent and has a strong case," he said. "This is a clear-cut wrongful arrest. With no prior criminal record, the worst-case scenario would be a slap on the hand."

"I hear what you're saying, but I didn't commit a crime. It would be wrong to plead guilty to something I didn't do. I am not a liar," I said.

What he neglected to tell me was that if I accepted the pre-trial offer, the arrest, and prosecution would have been deemed null and void as long as I stayed out of trouble. My case would be dismissed.

Beyond that, he didn't discuss the risks of going to trial, losing, and facing two to seven years behind bars. Instead, he focused on winning at trial, keeping my criminal record clean, and maintaining my reputation in the community. Had I known the truth, I wouldn't have gone to trial. Honestly, I don't believe any reasonable person would.

To make matters worse, the criminal charges came in addition to the other unresolved legal disputes related to the divorce that continued to filter through the court system. And there was still no resolution on the child support issue.

When Judge Greene stepped down from his Supreme Court role, a new judge, Judge Honore Dubois, was assigned to replace him. I knew very little about Judge Dubois at the time, except that he was a Willowbrook County Republican who had worked locally for over thirty years.

After a bit of digging, I found an article in the local paper that disclosed Judge Dubois had allegedly tried to conceal his financial interests in numerous lucrative residential development projects that required town approvals. The article generated such intense interest that the former Willowbrook County DA asked the state Attorney General's Office to investigate Dubois's business dealings.

To refresh your memory, after the pipe broke in our home and water ruined the kitchen and basement, I managed the repairs per the court order.

However, Judge Greene's order—signed just before he removed himself from the case—changed that, giving Darius the power to decide how to use the twenty-five-thousand-dollar insurance check. Based on Darius's handling of money in the past, I didn't trust him to do the right thing with the funds.

But Judge Dubois executed Greene's order by threatening me with (more) jail time for contempt of court if I didn't sign the check, hand it over to Darius, and depart the marital home.

When the town inspector declared the house in hazardous condition, it became obvious to me what I had to do. With no money and no job, I had no choice but to sign the check and hand it over to my attorney, who passed it on to Darius's attorney, who put the check—and our future—into Darius's hands. The kids and I left what had been our family home to stay in a hotel a few miles away while we waited for Darius to take care of completing the repairs.

The insurance company took care of hotel expenses and assured me in writing that the kids and I could stay there as long as necessary. They even alerted hotel management that Darius could not remove, cancel, or alter my stay, make any requests, or interact with them in any way.

We were there for three whole months before repairs were completed.

When it was finally time to leave the hotel, we had nowhere to go. I don't say that lightly. I mean, we honestly had nowhere. I was told that all our belongings had to be removed and that we were to move out so the house could be put on the market. To make things more complicated, I suffered a badly sprained my ankle on a skiing adventure with the kids. During the move, I could hardly walk, let alone carry boxes.

I didn't know what to do, so I prayed.

"Lord, we need a place to go," I said as tears dampened my cheeks. "I really need your help."

With my options dwindling, I stayed hyper-focused on any possible opportunities. One day, as I was picking my kids up from school, I noticed a handwritten sign on the side of the road announcing, "For Rent." I dialed the number indicated and set up an in-person interview. After checking the place out and having a pleasant conversation with the owner that same evening, I signed a short-term lease.

I moved our belongings from what had been the family home and never looked back.

The house sold a few weeks later for only two thousand dollars more than Darius and I had paid eleven years earlier.

"How could there be no equity in the place?" I asked my lawyer when I was told there would be little to no proceeds on the sale. "We've been paying down on the mortgage for eleven years."

"There was a thirty-thousand-dollar loan against the home," my attorney explained.

"What? How is that possible?" I asked. "I don't know anything about a loan being taken against the property. When was a loan taken out?"

"We could make a legal inquiry into the numbers," my lawyer suggested.

"Then we should do it," I said.

"It will cost you more money," he said, raising one eyebrow.

My lawyer knew I was tapped out.

"So, what you're telling me is that I get screwed again," I said in a disgusted tone.

On the upside, though, after six years, the only thing connecting Darius and me—aside from the kids— was the house, which was now sold.

"The closing costs were a little over ten thousand dollars, Maria. Darius has already paid his half. You owe the other half," the lawyer said matter-of-factly.

I got the raw end of the deal there, too.

While Judge Dubois replaced Judge Greene in the Supreme Court, Willowbrook County Family Court Support Magistrate Arbiter Olivia Blake was assigned to the post-divorce case in Family Court.

She would preside over the petition I filed in Family Court for unpaid spousal maintenance and the proper amount in child support.

If you are unfamiliar with this aspect of our legal system, Support Magistrates are attorneys chosen by a screening commission and appointed by the chief administrative judge. Their job is to hear child support and uncontested paternity matters.

"Darius's income has grown considerably to more than one hundred fifty-five thousand a year," I told my attorney. "There needs to be an adjustment."

I got busy pulling together the paperwork and submitted it to the courts.

"Mrs. Crowe has met the burden of proof. Mr. Crowe's income is well over the threshold for a modification in child support," Judge Blake announced.

The order was for more than double the amount previously assigned! I was ecstatic.

"This will make things much easier," I said excitedly, glancing at my lawyer and then back at the judge.

This time, Darius was ordered to make bi-weekly payments through the Support Collection Unit. He was also instructed to pay eighty-three percent of all unreimbursed medical expenses (as long as I provided receipts within thirty days) and outstanding dental expenses.

Blake's order that all payments be made through child support collections was significant—a huge victory, but more importantly, it offered some sense of financial security.

I had been fighting for this for years, and the victory felt incredible. For the first time since this whole thing started years early, I won!

Chapter Seven

TRIAL

"Injustice anywhere is a threat to justice everywhere."

~Martin Luther King Jr.

My criminal defense attorney often said, "New York State is a trial-by-ambush state." At the time, I did not understand what he meant, but after being subjected to the trial system, I totally got it.

I learned firsthand what he meant: When the system is working against you (or for your adversary), the truth doesn't really matter.

The criminal trial against me started on a Monday in Willowbrook County Supreme Court, located in the county's government seat, Brookfield Springs. The short fifteen-minute drive from my house to the courthouse each day was easy, but it seemed dismal.

Each morning before I left my house, my friend Jen came over to watch the kids.

"I'm not sure what to say to them," I whispered on the first day of my trial. "This whole thing seems so unreal—like I'm watching a movie or something."

She touched my hand and looked at me, her eyes misty with compassion.

"Look, Maria, you're a great mom. Once this whole thing is over, you can talk to them about it. In the meantime, I think it's important that you stay focused."

"I'm trying," I answered, looking wistfully into the living room where the kids were playing. They were so innocent and sweet. I felt sick thinking about the ramifications of all this drama going on in our lives. I had no idea what they understood, but they had to be feeling the stress.

Before the start of the trial, my attorney advised me that prosecutors had offered a late deal that would require me to plead guilty to a misdemeanor charge.

"That could be an option," I said. "If it goes on the record as a misdemeanor charge, I could tell my side of the story and regain my reputation, right?"

"Not necessarily. I suggest you reject the offer," he said without missing a beat.

I wasn't sure what to do. This wasn't my expertise, so I had no choice but to trust him.

Feeling a tightening in my gut, I said, "I'll do whatever you think is best. You are the expert, after all."

Until then, the most important thing I learned was that I knew very little about the system. I was at their mercy—my only recourse was to rely on the professionals. My attorney had years of experience in the system. He should have understood the ins and outs, so although I was nervous, I deferred to his opinion.

When the trial finally started, it lasted for three days. On day one, Darius and the lead investigator took the stand.

State Supreme Court Justice Reynolds III was assigned to the case. From my research, I knew that Reynolds was the son of a former mayor and the grandson of a United States congressman. I also learned that when he became a judge a few years earlier, by law, his first assistant became district attorney. The bottom line is that I was up against a district attorney's office that shared very close ties to the judge. I wondered if the relationship would affect the outcome of my trial.

DAY ONE: MONDAY, MAY 16, 2016

JUDGE: Please put your hand on the Holy Bible. Do you swear to tell the truth, the whole truth, and nothing but the truth, so help you God?

DARIUS: Yes, I do, Your Honor.

ADA: How do you know Maria?

DARIUS: She's my ex-wife.

ADA: Is she in the courtroom today?

DARIUS: She is.

ADA: And what was the defendant's address in July of 2013?

DARIUS: 7 Maplewood Lane, Meadow Park. We both still owned it.

ADA: Can you describe the circumstances surrounding your discovery of the insurance check and how you got a copy of the check?

DARIUS: I went to the bank one day, and there was a teller. I don't remember her name, but it was a woman. I explained the situation, and she gave me a copy of the check.

ADA: I'm going to draw your attention to the back of that check. How many signatures do you see on that?

DARIUS: Two.

ADA: OK, now sir, that signature that appears on the top there, is that your signature?

DARIUS: I didn't sign it. But it looks like it was intended to be my signature.

ADA: OK. Why would you say that?

DARIUS: Well, I sign my name sometimes as...I don't know which one I should point to.

ADA: If you can point over here to this one, sir.

DARIUS: Pardon me, I drank too much coffee. The D, I do kind of looping, which is like that one there. It's similar in style.

MY ATTORNEY: Your Honor, I'm objecting. We're delving into analysis here.

JUDGE: Overruled.

ADA: When you are looking at the signature, does it appear someone was trying to make it appear as your signature?

DARIUS: Yes.

ADA: Can you tell us what this check was intended for?

DARIUS: Yep. In my conversation with the insurance company, they provided me with the information about the check and the claim that was made. It was for damage to the siding on the house.

ADA: OK. I have no further questions, Your Honor.

JUDGE: Cross-examination.

It was my attorney's moment to confront Darius. I was looking forward to his cross-examination since on multiple occasions, he spoke of his eagerness to get to the truth. He said he was looking forward to "destroying" him.

ATTORNEY: Thank you, Judge. What was the date that your divorce was finalized?

DARIUS: September of 2013.

ATTORNEY: OK, so in June of 2013, you weren't living in the house on Maplewood Lane, correct?

DARIUS: I was not.

ATTORNEY: Was it your house, was it Maria's house, or was it both of yours?

DARIUS: We both owned the house still.

ATTORNEY: Maria lived there, correct?

DARIUS: Correct.

ATTORNEY: You weren't responsible for the maintenance of the house, correct?

DARIUS: Correct.

ATTORNEY: When you were going through the divorce in 2013, is it correct that what was to be determined with the house wasn't completed yet? You were in court, right?

DARIUS: We were still in court, correct?

ATTORNEY: Did you have any agreements regarding the house at this time, any separation agreement, or any directives from the Court?

DARIUS: I was paying for the mortgage, the insurance, and the taxes.

ATTORNEY: OK. Ultimately, more than three years went by, and you were unaware of even the existence of this check?

DARIUS: Correct.

ATTORNEY: OK. Now, you called the insurance company and they gave you documentation as to what the claim was about?

DARIUS: Correct.

ATTORNEY: And they did that because you were still on the policy, correct?

DARIUS: Correct.

ATTORNEY: And you were to remain on the policy until the house was sold?

DARIUS: Right. I was still paying the policy.

ATTORNEY: Are you out of any out-of-pocket expenses as a result of this check?

DARIUS: Was money taken from me as a result of this check or...

ATTORNEY: Have you suffered any financial loss as a result of that check?

DARIUS: I think you could say I am, yeah. This check, again, I don't know what it was used for. I know what it was intended for. And...

ATTORNEY: Hold on. I asked if you were out of any financial loss.

DARIUS: Right.

ATTORNEY: Were you out a financial loss?

DARIUS: Well, you want my explanation or...

ATTORNEY: I'd like a yes or a no.

DARIUS: OK. Um, I think it's possible because the money still had to be spent. There were other claims for other losses that had to be spread around...

ATTORNEY: After you received this check, became aware of it, what did you do next?

DARIUS: One of my first steps was to contact my ex-wife.

ATTORNEY: You knew you were coming here today to testify. Are you claiming that you're out of money as a result of this check?

DARIUS: That was not the claim, no.

ATTORNEY: So, ultimately, you went to the police, correct?

DARIUS: Correct.

ATTORNEY: New York State Police in Meadow Park?

DARIUS: Correct.

ATTORNEY: To the barracks where you work?

DARIUS: Correct.

ATTORNEY: And you were dealing with a specific trooper?

DARIUS: Yes.

ATTORNEY: And you went to him, why?

DARIUS: Because he's the lead investigator.

ATTORNEY: OK. You felt you were the victim of a crime?

DARIUS: Yes.

ATTORNEY: OK. And again, as a result of this check, what was your loss?

DARIUS: Well...

ADA: Objection. Asked and answered.

JUDGE: Overruled. Answer the question.

DARIUS: It's the loss anybody would sustain after having their signature forged and check deposited that they are not aware of with funds more than $1,000. I mean, it's ... call it identity theft, whatever you want. I don't know.

ATTORNEY: When you looked into this claim, were you aware of any deductibles? Are you familiar with your insurance policy?

DARIUS: Sure.

ATTORNEY: Would you agree with me that on that claim with this check, this is the figure minus the $1,000 deductible?

DARIUS: I'd have to go back and look at the policy.

ATTORNEY: I'm going to hand you what's been marked as Defendant's Exhibit A, ask that you look at it and when you're done reviewing that document, please let me know if you recognize that document.

DARIUS: Yep. Sure, now that I see it. Yeah, I recall this now.

ATTORNEY: Do you agree or do you disagree that there was a $1,000 deductible?

DARIUS: There was, yep.

ATTORNEY: Thank you. Nothing further.

Darius was excused.

Nothing further? That's it? What happened to grilling him? What happened to "destroying" him? I thought as I tried to control my anger. My attorney had led me to believe he would expose Darius for the liar that he was. Instead, he played into the Willowbrook game.

The ADA stood up and called the State Police investigator to the stand.

ADA: What are your duties and responsibilities with The New York State Police?

INVESTIGATOR: Currently, I am assigned to the Major Crimes Unit in Limoux. At the time of this case, I was assigned to Meadow Park barracks with the Bureau of Criminal Investigations, where I was responsible primarily for conducting felony-level investigations and crimes against children.

ADA: I'm going to ask you to draw attention to June 3, 2014. Did you become involved in an investigation regarding a check that was deposited at the Meadow Park branch of Willowcrest Financial Institution?

INVESTIGATOR: I was.

ADA: Can you describe the circumstances of how you became involved in that investigation?

INVESTIGATOR: Darius Crowe contacted our office to report that there was a series of checks that had been deposited into a joint Summit Grove Credit Union account that had been in his name, and now was in his ex-wife's name. He learned of these checks being deposited into the joint account.

ADA: Now, what did you do as a result of receiving this information?

INVESTIGATOR: Initially, I checked with the underwriter for Prudential Insurance to get some background as far as the checks. Once we established that one of the checks, the one of July 2013, had been transacted at Willowcrest Financial Institution, I went to that location to see if they had surveillance footage and then also to find Maria Crowe.

ADA: OK. And did you ever determine whose signature was the top signature?

INVESTIGATOR: I interviewed Darius. He indicated that he was not the person that signed it. And being that the only two people that would be authorized to sign the check are himself and his ex-wife, he indicated that that was a forged signature on the top.

ADA: OK. Now, you are not a handwriting expert, are you?

INVESTIGATOR: No.

ADA: OK. Did you do anything in furtherance of comparing that signature to anything, just to determine what, if anything, it was?

INVESTIGATOR: I did have a copy, or a deposition, that was filed by Darius in the course of this investigation. I did compare them to one another.

ATTORNEY: Judge, I'm going to object. He's indicated he's not an expert in handwriting analysis.

JUDGE: Overruled. I'll let the jury hear the testimony and consider it for what it's worth. Go ahead, Investigator.

INVESTIGATOR: I did do a comparison of the signature from the deposition to the signatures on the rear portion of the check.

ADA: OK. And what, if anything, was your conclusion, as an investigator, with regard to those signatures?

INVESTIGATOR: That they were not the same, that it was not Darius's signature from what I could tell.

ADA: OK. Did it look similar?

INVESTIGATOR: It had...

ATTORNEY: Same objection.

JUDGE: Overruled.

INVESTIGATOR: There were certain portions of it that did have some similarities, yes.

ADA: Now, on July 30, 2014, what was the nature of the discussion with the defendant?

INVESTIGATOR: Maria had come to the State Police barracks looking to make a report against her ex-husband.

ADA: And did you end up discussing anything with regard to this case?

INVESTIGATOR: Not on July 30.

The judge suddenly interjected and made a directive to the jurors.

JUDGE: Before we go on, we'll take a break in just a few seconds. A few questions ago, though, (the defense attorney) objected to a question by the ADA relative to the investigator's comparison of handwriting from the check in an unidentified document. I overruled the objection and allowed the answer. In retrospect, I think that was an improper ruling on my part. I am going to reverse my ruling, sustain the objection, and strike the answer for the record.

So, this is one of those un-ring-the-bell examples. You've heard the answer. I'm directing you that you cannot consider the document. The investigator is not a handwriting expert. Alright, I think we will take a 15-minute break at this point. During the break, don't discuss the case, don't deliberate about the case. We'll be with you shortly, but this will be the afternoon break before we break for the day. OK? Thank you.

**I would like to note here that the Judge admitted he made a mistake by allowing the document to be seen in the first place. But do you think you could forget something you just saw and heard? In my opinion, it would be impossible. **

Criminal trials are high-stakes affairs, but they are also remarkably sterile. Imagine deciding between tuna salad or peanut butter and jelly for lunch when your freedom is on the line.

"How am I supposed to eat?" I asked. My stomach was tied in knots, and I already felt sick. Adding food to the turbulence in my gut would be asking for trouble.

"Maria, you need to keep your strength up," my attorney said. "It's going to be a long afternoon."

I nibbled on a few crackers and sipped on some water. Once everyone was back in their seats, the proceedings started again.

ADA: Did you charge Maria with anything regarding those checks?

INVESTIGATOR: The ones at Summit Grove Credit Union?

ADA: Yes.

INVESTIGATOR: No.

ADA: Why not?

INVESTIGATOR: On those particular checks, there were three checks. There was one that just had the name of Maria that was signed on the back of it. There was another one that had Maria Crowe and Maria Fatima Crowe, which, it's my understanding that's her maiden name. And then the last check had Maria Crowe, and what appeared to be the initials of MC, which I took to be from Maria Crowe. So, on those particular checks, there were no forged signatures.

ADA: Now, after listening to that tape, there were quite a few accusations thrown at Darius as far as potential criminal activity. Did you look into any of those accusations?

INVESTIGATOR: No.

ADA: Did you eventually charge Maria with anything?

INVESTIGATOR: Yes.

ADA: Did you ever charge Darius with anything?

INVESTIGATOR: No.

ADA: And what did you charge Maria with?

INVESTIGATOR: Criminal possession of a forged instrument in the second degree.

ADA: And what transaction was that in relation to?

INVESTIGATOR: That was the check that was transacted at the Willowcrest Financial Institution.

The ADA thanked the investigator and told the court that he had no more questions. My attorney approached the investigator for cross-examination.

ATTORNEY: First off, I want to ask you about the audio recording that we just listened to. When you made that recording, did you inform Maria that you were recording the call?

INVESTIGATOR: No.

ATTORNEY: Had you spoken to her in person prior to this call?

INVESTIGATOR: I had not, no.

ATTORNEY: So, she didn't know why you were calling, correct?

INVESTIGATOR: No.

ATTORNEY: Now, I want to talk to you about the Willowcrest Financial Institution. Darius came to you with a complaint about banking with his ex-wife, or wife at the time, I should say. Or were they divorced when he met you?

INVESTIGATOR: When he made the report, um, it's my understanding they were divorced at that time.

ATTORNEY: So, they were divorced at that time, but he's complaining about checks from about a year earlier. Is that correct, a year or so?

INVESTIGATOR: Correct.

ATTORNEY: Take a look at this check... is it your opinion that this is a forged signature?

INVESTIGATOR: Yes.

ATTORNEY: So, is it your testimony that, which line is it that you believe is the forgery?

INVESTIGATOR: The top one.

ATTORNEY: You previously mentioned that you looked for video footage, and there was none available to you.

INVESTIGATOR: Correct.

ATTORNEY: Why is that?

INVESTIGATOR: They hold the footage for about six months.

ATTORNEY: And isn't it correct that this check was from when they were still married? From 2013, almost three years ago?

INVESTIGATOR: Yes.

ATTORNEY: That's all I have. Thank you, Investigator.

My attorney made a motion to dismiss for the People's failure to support evidence, including the element of intent, the same motion he made pre-trial.

ATTORNEY: Judge, the People introduced evidence of Maria by the way of a recorded telephone conversation, where she clearly indicates that the funds were used to fix the marital home. Additionally, the complainant, or so-called 'victim' in this matter, took the stand and testified today that he could not testify to any out-of-pocket loss or how this affected him. So, I think the element of intent is necessary. And also Judge, in terms of providing for a forgery, we just heard from the investigator, who gets on the stand and pretends to be a writing expert based on his opinion. So, I find it very difficult going forward as a matter of law, Judge, that the People have introduced any evidence to support intent, and also to support the fact based on the investigator's testimony that we are even dealing with forgery. So, Judge, I am asking the court to review the evidence and the law here about whether or not this document... it's my position as a matter of law that this document is not a forged signature; number one and number two, the People have failed to show any malcontent, any harm, or any intent to defraud, deceive, or injure. So, I think the People have failed on both the law and intent in this case, and I ask that the sole count of the indictment be dismissed.

At the end of the day, I drove home and cried—a lot. Anyone else would have done the same. The experience had been emotionally draining. These people and the jury had my future and my life in their hands.

After kissing my kids goodnight, it was pretty clear that falling asleep would be impossible. I paced through the house for a while before reaching out to media outlets as far as Metropolis Heights, a town about fifty miles away. I needed to tell my side of the story.

"Please, no one will listen to me," I said when I got a previous colleague on the line. "Would you at least give me five minutes to tell my side of the story?" I begged.

His response felt like a hard slap in the face.

"Maria, I'm worried about you. You've always been such a great reporter, but it feels like you're losing it," he said.

On one level, he was right; I was losing it. I had already lost so much and had so much more to lose. To date, I had lost my reputation and my livelihood. Now, I was losing faith in what, up until then, I believed was a justice system. Plus, I was terrified that I was going to lose my freedom for something I didn't do, and I was horrified thinking about the possibility of losing my kids.

The bigger networks told me that they wouldn't be able to cover the story unless something really bad happened, like me going to jail.

Bullshit! I thought. I became a journalist because I wanted to reveal both sides of any story. In my mind, it was my job, and the job of every other journalist on the planet, to shine the light where light needed to be shone. Criminals were being let off with a slap on the hand, but a mother of three kids, who had done nothing wrong, was being abused by the system. Why wouldn't these supposed journalists at least listen to my story? This was all such a sham.

On the last day of the trial, I hugged my kids hard, kissing the tops of their heads. The expression on my daughter's face was something I will never forget. I could feel her fear and vulnerability. What would happen to her if her mother didn't come home?

My heart still hurts when I think back on that morning.

DAY TWO: TUESDAY, MAY 17, 2016

JUDGE: Good morning. Yesterday, I reversed a ruling that (the Defense) had objected to regarding a conclusion that the police investigator made relative to the forgery. As you will recall, testimony was stricken from the record and must be disregarded. I would propose an additional sentence that says, 'It is not in evidence, and it is to be disregarded by you.'

I am still flabbergasted that the judge made the mistake in the first place. And then to off-handedly tell the jury to forget what happened was ludicrous. How was the jury supposed to forget?

Summation

ATTORNEY: Ladies and gentlemen, it's Wednesday. It wasn't a very long trial because there wasn't much evidence. Early on, an ADA indicated that he would have no expert, no scientist, and no video. He was right, and it's probably the only thing we will agree on.

He didn't have any of those things. They had no video, now I think there's a very good explanation to that... it was in 2013. We are now in 2016. Banks don't keep video that long, but why did they not have expert witnesses or a scientist?

This is their case to prove. In a few short moments, these government prosecutors are going to stand up and ask you to convict my client of a crime, a felony. We heard from the manager of the bank. She told you that the bank has a policy against taking a check made out to two people and depositing it into one account. Why did the manager of the bank override that rule? You heard the manager's testimony. They looked at the back of the check, saw the writing on the back. No problem. Even though they knew it was made out to two people, the bank put it into one. The bank allowed this to happen, right or wrong.

My client is not charged with forgery. The People are running this prosecution. You heard the tape from the State Police investigator. My client said she signed the check. Well, we didn't get a forgery charge. What else wasn't charged in this case? A larceny, stealing? We've heard Darius indicate he has experienced no loss. This is all your evidence. This is all that you have. All of it is your so-called evidence. Now, these prosecutors are going to stand in front of you and ask you to convict Maria on the totality of the 'evidence,' or lack of evidence.

Then we heard from Darius. I think Maria's tape explains a lot about the relationship between these parties. Their divorce wasn't pleasant. Now, we have the house itself. We all know Darius wasn't living there. Maria was responsible for taking care of it. You heard Maria saying on the tape that there was a problem with the house; there was damage, and when she got the insurance check, she fixed it.

The People have failed to show that this is a crime. Not only do these prosecutors need to prove that the instrument itself was forged, but they don't need to prove who forged it because they didn't charge that. They only need to prove that it was forged. They've got to provide you with some evidence to rely on. Darius didn't sign it. Does that necessarily mean that his signature was forged? I don't think so. The Police investigator makes a conclusion based on his opinion that it's forged. He admits he is not an expert on handwriting. The People have not presented a handwriting expert. If you want a criminal conviction under our law, the prosecutor needs to earn it. It is their burden, and they must prove it beyond a reasonable doubt. This case was nothing but shortcuts. They prosecuted it like a no-seatbelt ticket. In other words, they didn't prosecute it. They are going to stand in front of you and ask you to convict this woman of a felony. They didn't do their job.

VERDICT

JUDGE: Good afternoon, Mr. Foreperson, have you reached a verdict?

FOREPERSON: Yes, Your Honor.

The court officer received the verdict from the foreperson and handed it to the judge. The judge read it silently and returned it to the foreperson. I felt as though my heart stopped beating. I felt as if my whole body was numb as my mind struggled to wrap itself around what was real and what wasn't. The scene playing out in front of me reminded me of an old CSI episode, one where the plaintiff was wrongly accused.

JUDGE: Would the defendant please rise? As to the count of criminal possession of a forged instrument in the second degree, how do you find?

FOREPERSON: We, the Jury, find the defendant guilty.

JUDGE: Does either side wish the jury polled?

My attorney turned to me to say, "If they are going to declare you guilty, they will have to say it to your face."

ATTORNEY: Yes, Your Honor.

JUDGE: Please poll the Jury.

One by one, the jurors were asked to state their decision. I met each of their eyes as they spoke.

"Guilty." "Guilty." "Guilty." Guilty." "Guilty." "Guilty." "Guilty." "Guilty."

I will never forget my attorney's face. His jaw literally dropped as the poll continued.

"Guilty." "Guilty." "Guilty." "Guilty."

The judge thanked the jury for their service before excusing them. Everyone stood up as they exited the room, and the judge pounded the gavel to quiet the hubbub that had arisen.

JUDGE: I am remanding the defendant to the custody of Willowbrook County Sheriff's Department without bail until sentencing on July 19th.

ATTORNEY: Judge, I would like to be heard regarding your remand, if I may?

My attorney reiterated that I had a spotless record and that the judge's decision was not fair or the right thing to do.

JUDGE: The defendant faces up to 2 1/3 to 7 years in State Prison. She has lived outside of the country in Cordova for an extended period of time. I believe that the risk of flight is great. I deny your application. I am remanding her to the custody of the sheriff at this time. That will conclude the matter. I'll see you on July 19th at 9:30 a.m.

I was to be sent to jail without the option of bail.

Suddenly, even though the courthouse was loud and chaotic, I could hear the sound of my own breathing. My heartbeat was slow and peaceful. I could only describe it as an out-of-body experience or as if I was watching a movie where someone else, a woman who looked just like me, was playing the main character. It felt unreal, but what was happening was very, *very* real.

"WOW, what?!?" my attorney said in shocked dismay. I will never forget his expression—his eyes looked as though they would pop from the sockets, and his face and lips resembled that of a carp when it's been pulled from the water.

(Honestly, I felt bad for him even though I was the one being sent to jail. It was obvious that he hadn't expected the verdict that was passed down.)

ATTORNEY: Your Honor, her children are waiting for her to come home. She is an obedient citizen with no record.

JUDGE: She's a flight risk.

ATTORNEY: WHAT?

I looked at my attorney and calmly said, "It's OK."

A blond officer, whom I had seen in Family Court numerous times, approached me and said, "Maria, we have to go."

I handed my belongings to a friend—a purse, a sandwich bag with good luck slime given to me by my youngest daughter, a paper flower with little love notes made and given to me by my older daughter, and my cell phone.

Taking a deep breath, I straightened myself up and looked around at everyone sitting behind me.

"Darius wins again in Willowbrook County," I said, walking past the judge without looking at him. I couldn't believe he would do something like this to me, and I refused to give him the satisfaction of seeing me in pain.

Karma's a bitch, I thought. *He'll get his one day.*

Another officer I had seen several times asked concernedly, "Maria, are you alright?"

"Yes," I answered.

I probably looked stoic, or maybe I appeared to him in the moment to resemble a robot devoid of emotion.

I was led to a small cell located behind the courtroom, where I sat on a wooden bench with my hands folded. For the first time since I arrived at the courthouse that day, I was alone.

In a moment of clarity, I surrendered to my circumstances. This was not about control—it was about faith. I closed my eyes and made a solemn promise to God.

"Your will be done. I'm here to serve You. I'm here to do what You want me to do. I don't have any control over any of this, and I promise You that I will not lose faith or blame You. Please help me; give me the strength and knowledge to endure this."

I sat there for a good hour before a female officer searched me for drugs or weapons. She was kind when she said, "I'm sorry, but I am going to have to handcuff you. I need you to turn around."

Once more, I saw the whole situation as if it were happening to someone else. I had never in my life imagined myself handcuffed, but here I was, the metal cuffs biting slightly into my wrists.

The heels I wore to court that day clicked down the stairs and outside where the sheriff's car door was open. I slid without a word onto the hard back seat. The space was very tight, and it hurt sitting with my hands cuffed behind my back. The waterworks started as the reality of the situation hit me. So many emotions roiled through my body as I wondered how someone could be so sick as to do this to a woman he had supposedly loved.

As I rode toward the jail, I recalled the dozens of professionals, parents, and parishioners who had written character references for me to the judge. The notes testified that I had served the community for many years and posed no threat. One in particular played through my mind.

"Maria is a person who always exudes positive energy. She creates an atmosphere of excitement and achievement wherever she goes. Maria is the epitome of a "can-do" person. She's a natural leader, and she never takes shortcuts."

Those letters of support had meant the world to me, and I believed they had the potential to show the judge that I prided myself on being a person of character.

My attorney told me that he had forwarded the letters to the court. However, later on, he admitted that he had only delivered one.

This was the same attorney who adamantly advised me not to testify on my own behalf. He was right that I have no experience with the courts, but I'm a professional communicator. I would have presented a clear and cogent testimony if I had been properly coached.

Instead, I was on my way to jail.

Chapter Eight

ISOLATION

"The only thing necessary for the triumph of evil is for good men to do nothing."

~Edmund Burke

Memorial Day weekend marks the unofficial start of summer, but I definitely did not feel like partying while locked away in a jail cell for a crime I didn't commit.

I spent the holiday sitting by myself in cell 113, hoping and praying that the judge could be convinced to grant me bail. How could I plan my defense if I was locked up?

Meanwhile, my ex-husband, who was more than likely enjoying a picnic at the lake with his new family, had days earlier submitted a petition to terminate child support payments. I could almost hear his triumphant voice.

With her locked up, why would she need support payments?

I had hoped a bail hearing would be held on Friday, but it was postponed until the Tuesday after Memorial Day.

"But that means it will be held the same morning as the bail hearing. How does that work?" I asked my attorney.

"Don't worry, Maria. We'll make it work," he said.

I wasn't sure I believed him. It was bad enough that I was in jail, where I was struggling to adjust to the stark environment. I felt cold most of the time and was overwhelmed by waves of anxiety, followed by deeper waves of desperation. Under the circumstances, I think anyone would have been feeling the same way. So much had already been taken away, and there was more to lose.

My mind ran nonstop, a hamster wheel of repeating thoughts. I was tortured by worries about my kids. How would this experience affect them? Would there be long-term ramifications? I couldn't imagine there wouldn't be. What a terrible thing for a child to have to experience knowing their mom was taken away in handcuffs for "doing something bad."

The memory of the expression of fear and worry on my youngest daughter's face as I left for the court that last day crippled me. Somehow, I felt I had let them down. I knew it wasn't my fault, but how would they ever understand the travesty that was being committed against me by what I had always thought of as our justice system?

Throughout the process, I met other moms who suffered similar travesties at the hands of what was supposed to be a justice system.

I had been warned by a psychologist not to talk to the kids about what was going on. Plus, I didn't want them to feel like they were in the middle. I did my best even when the favor was not returned from Darius.

I can't even defend myself to them, I thought. *Will they even believe me when I tell them my side of the story?*

I felt sick thinking that, after a while, my case would be a distant memory. Everyone involved would move on with their lives as though it had never happened, and maybe occasionally, my name would come up.

Whatever happened to that Maria Crowe? Is she still in jail?

The thought sent shivers down my spine.

Then, an even more horrific thought blasted into my mind. *Would my kids even remember me? Would they remember the fun we had together?*

Memories of braiding my daughter's hair as the morning sun filtered through the kitchen window almost made me cry.

"Mommy, I love you to the moon," she said.

"I love you to infinity and beyond," I responded as my fingers ran through her dark curls.

"You do?" she asked, glancing to the side to bring me into her peripheral view.

"I do," I answered.

"How much is that?" she asked.

"THIS much more," I answered, spreading my arms wide before wrapping them around her and hugging her hard.

The resonant echoes of giggles caused a reflexive jolt, making my stomach clench.

I can't think about them, I thought. God, I need your help. How do I deal with this grief?

Quickly, I realized I would need to focus on a time before any of this happened. Memories flashed through my mind, and I settled on imagining myself back in college—working toward the beautiful life I would create when I finished.

It wasn't easy to stay there, though. Less than twelve months earlier, I had been crowned National Miss, and now I was playing ping pong under the stark light of an unshaded light bulb in a jail rec room.

"How does a divorce case end up like this?" both guards and inmates asked.

"If I had a clue, I wouldn't be here," I answered. I appreciated their concern, and it made me feel better that they saw the insanity that landed me there.

The Saturday evening before Memorial Day, I made popcorn while another inmate retrieved a bag of trail mix. After combining our snacks in a big bowl, we decided to have a picnic and play some UNO.

"You can't do that!" I laughed as the game started to get silly.

"Yes, I can!" my opponent insisted, her grin wide and her eyes twinkling.

"No, you can't!" By now, I was laughing so hard my stomach hurt. "Oh, my God, it feels so good to laugh! I don't remember the last time I laughed like this!" I admitted, wiping my eyes.

The laughter was a short but much-appreciated reprieve from the ongoing onslaught of worry. Most of the time, I couldn't help but feel as though my life was ruined. How could I bounce back from an experience like this?

My career had been devastated, and without it, I hadn't yet figured out what to do for work to support myself and the kids. I needed a plan to get my life back together, but I was too stressed out and tired to even think about what life after jail time might look like.

It seemed that my only option was to give it all to God.

"I feel you here," I often whispered into my quiet cell. I had no doubt that He was listening, and a deep knowing gave me confidence that my situation would be resolved in a positive way, even though I had no idea how that might happen.

Early that Sunday, my sleep was interrupted by an officer screaming at the top of her lungs.

"WAKE UP! STAND BY YOUR DOOR!"

I hadn't slept much the previous night as repeating thoughts kept up a steady drum beat in my head.

At breakfast, I listlessly chewed toast that I washed down with apple juice. As I prepared to take a shower, I went downstairs to ask the guard for a razor so I could shave my legs. My cousin was coming for a visit, so I wanted to feel good about my appearance. I stood there for several minutes while the guard chit-chatted with a couple of women I hadn't seen before. I cleared my throat several times, but she ignored me, acting as if she didn't see me.

"Fuck the razor!" I whispered loudly before heading back upstairs to a hot shower.

I vividly remember thinking the weather was perfect for a holiday weekend: warm and sunny with a slight breeze. I imagined everyone I knew at the lake, laughing, eating burgers and hot dogs, and maybe even dipping their feet into the still chilly water.

Is anyone thinking about me? I wondered, my heart plunging at the idea that they weren't.

But my cousin, who was my childhood buddy, paid me a visit that day.

"Oh, my God, I'm so happy to see you," I said, crying as we hugged.

"You look good. I love your hair," she said, indicating the fancy bun I had pulled my long locks into after my shower. "They let you do that in here?"

"You should see what else they let us do in here," I said, winking. She giggled and hugged me again.

What she didn't know was that I had gotten "dolled up," if only to make the visit less painful for her.

I continued joking around to keep things light. I guess it was my way of keeping her comfortable in an uncomfortable situation.

Her visit gave me a much-needed boost. It was something to hang onto, but it was too short. After all, time flies when we are with people we love.

We hugged hard as she was getting ready to go.

"I'll see you soon," she said.

"You absolutely will," I said, squeezing her hand as she turned to go. I closed my eyes and whispered, "I will be home soon."

After the visit, a female guard took me into a side room to do a search. I knew it was protocol, but I still wasn't comfortable with stripping down to nothing and standing naked in front of a stranger.

"Squat and cough," she said nonchalantly.

I tilted my head quizzically and said, "I'm sorry. I don't understand what you want me to do."

"Squat down and cough like this," she said, dropping into position and mimicking a cough.

"Do people actually shove stuff up there?" I asked after doing what I was told.

"Oh, YES, they do," she said.

Once more fully dressed, I returned to my cell, where I sat down to pray that the next day's court session would send me home to my children. When Job lost everything, God gave him double. I set my heart on that ending.

Let me take you back to two days before my trial commenced when, in a miraculous turn of events, I sought counsel from an Appeals Attorney who came recommended by a friend.

"He specializes exclusively in appeals," my friend said.

He turned out to be wonderful, quickly and astutely, highlighting the injustice pervading Willowbrook County Family Court.

"It is critical that your criminal defense counsel be adequately prepared," he said before advising that all necessary documents for a bail application be filed in advance in case of an unfavorable trial outcome. Armed with this insight, I made a call to my attorney.

"We need to brace for the worst-case scenario," I said after sharing what I had learned.

Still, believe it or not, even though my attorney saw and understood the judge's apparent bias against me, he showed up at court without the necessary paperwork.

It wasn't until seven agonizing days into my jail term that my criminal defense attorney finally made an appearance.

Despite repeated attempts to reach him, including a dear friend of mine paying my attorney a visit at his office, I still heard nothing.

"He's away on vacation," my friend reported.

"What? Are you kidding me?" I asked, shocked. "Didn't he leave anyone else to handle my case?"

"Apparently not," he answered.

When my attorney finally returned, I begged him to file the necessary paperwork for my bail hearing.

MONDAY, MAY 30th – Memorial Day

The bail hearing was set for 9 a.m. the next day, with the Family Court hearing to deal with Darius's petition to cancel child support an hour later.

Monday evening, hoping not to return to jail after my hearing on Tuesday, I gave my jail possessions to a woman who had become my friend.

I thanked God for supporting me while I was there and for helping me cope with the resulting anxiety. I thanked Him for good friends, without whom I wouldn't have lasted. Then I thanked everyone there for the food, the clothes, and most importantly, the time spent laughing. After lights out, I prayed for each of them to find peace and a better life. And I prayed all night for a positive outcome. I needed to get home to my kids.

TUESDAY, MAY 31st

By morning, I realized I was coming to grips with having no control.

No matter how hard you or I try to exert control over our destiny, in certain situations, we have none. I was at the mercy of the system at that point. I felt powerless to change my fate. I surrendered control and hoped for the best. I needed to prepare for anything. I would trust God.

Before leaving the jail for court, I asked the deputies if I could wear civilian clothes. I didn't want to give Darius the satisfaction of seeing me in chains, and I definitely didn't need the judges to see me dressed like a criminal.

Members of the sheriff's staff treated me fairly, but the law prevented them from allowing me to appear in civilian clothing. If the judge set bail and I paid it, deputies assured me they would take me back to the jail to change and retrieve my belongings.

Deputies did, however, offer me the option of wearing pink handcuffs.

"Really? Thank you so much," I said, finding the whole idea humorous even if it wasn't funny. But the sheriff's staff liked me and were always respectful, telling me I was the only "normal" person in there. I appreciated their kindness.

The handcuffs were attached to chains wrapped around my waist and ankles. I stood before the judges in green jail garb, chains, and Crocs.

In an incredible turnaround, Justice Reynolds, who less than two weeks ago had called me a flight risk and rejected my bail request, ordered me free on four thousand dollars bail. I would need to stay out of trouble, which would be easy since I never committed a crime in the first place. A sentencing date was set.

It should have been time to celebrate, but I still faced the trumped-up felony charge. Plus, I had immediate concerns in Family Court.

The walk to Family Court was short—directly across the courtyard from the Supreme Court building where my bail hearing had just taken place.

Tears flooded my cheeks as I stood before the imposing doors of the Supreme Court, flanked by two armed sheriffs. My heart was pounding, and I was feeling frantic. I didn't want Darius or anyone else seeing me like this. It was all so wrong. I was an upstanding citizen. I had always worked hard and loved hard. I was not a criminal, and I didn't deserve to be treated like one.

"Can you please remove my handcuffs?" I begged, desperation flooding my voice. Feeling unable to fathom the humiliation of crossing the courtyard looking like a criminal, their apologies did little to soothe me even though I understood that while I was bound by handcuffs and the heavy weight of missing my children, they were bound by the constraints of the law.

Each step forward brought visions of Jesus enduring the torment of carrying his cross to Golgotha, where he would be crucified. Every beat of my heart bore the same agony of his journey—an unjustified sentence carried out on an innocent person.

With the reluctant assistance of the sheriffs, I crossed the atrium, each footstep a testament to the resilience forged in adversity.

From where I stood, I felt all eyes on me, and I could feel Darius's burning into my back. The court eventually emptied, and my case was called.

Darius had no clue that I had just attended a bail hearing and was about to be released from jail. He fully expected the judge to waive his child support responsibilities because he believed I wouldn't be returning home.

I wish I could have seen the look of shock on his face when the sheriff's deputies informed Family Court that I had been granted bail and was prepared to post it. The Magistrate, who had appeared ready to side with Darius, instantly dismissed the petition.

Both shared custody and child support were reinstated upon my release that day.

It all worked out with impeccable timing. Darius shot me a glaring look as we exited the court. He opened the door and held it for a few seconds, glancing back at me with a smirk as if he were deliberately provoking a reaction.

"Ignore him," the sheriff advised.

I had every intention of doing just that. I held my head up high as I shuffled to the sheriff's car for the ride to pick up my belongings.

My freedom was temporary and based on probationary supervision, which meant I had to strictly adhere to the law and report to a probation officer weekly. I also had to resist the urge to react to Darius's provocations.

With sentencing scheduled for seven weeks later, I decided to avoid contact with most people. I would live a quiet, secluded life with my kids.

I found a job at a local construction company as an executive assistant and marketing director. At the time, I felt a little trapped in the office position—I was a creative person, not an accountant. But my boss, the company's owner, hired me despite my legal problems.

He was a supportive man, even writing a letter of reference urging the judge not to sentence me to jail time.

One day, while I was at work, a process server arrived and delivered court papers notifying me that

Darius had filed a new modification petition with the court, this one seeking a reduction in monthly child support.

"He's such a loser," I told my friend that night. "Can you imagine him having me served at work? It's just another slimy attempt to sabotage me. I don't understand why he hates me so much."

Luckily, my boss brushed it off.

I attended Bible study regularly. I prayed with the other attendees about my sentencing. Sometimes, I jerked awake at night as the dark shadow of premonition permeated my dream time.

"Give up your anxieties to God. You know He hears you. He will help work everything out for you," they said.

At that point, I had almost no money and owed tens of thousands of dollars in lawyer fees. Darius had walked out five years earlier, and I was tired of trying to fix what I had no control over. So, I prayed.

Sentencing

I woke up the morning of my sentencing with a feeling that could only be described as complete dread. At the same time, though, I wanted to get it over with. I prayed that things would work out in my favor, but experience taught me that the outcome was questionable. I wasn't confident that I would be coming back home.

My parents were out of the country, but four good friends, priests from my church, Bible study group members, and my construction company boss came to support me at sentencing. I was feeling so beaten down that I felt nothing when the judge announced the sentence.

This time, I came to court prepared. On my arm were written the names and phone numbers of everyone I would need if I were sent to jail again—attorneys, the kids' doctors, and my cousin Devina.

As I stood in front of the judge, I got the strong sense that he didn't like the fact that I showed up as a confident woman.

The proceeding immediately turned hostile and took a worrisome but not unexpected turn when the ADA argued that I deserved jail time.

"Given that Ms. Crowe has no prior record, I thought probation may be appropriate," the prosecutor told the court before adding that my behavior and refusal to accept responsibility had convinced him otherwise.

"The People are recommending a sentence of six months' incarceration to be followed by five years' probation," the ADA said. He noted that I had filed a complaint about the State Police, insisting the investigator who handled the case acted in an "extremely professional manner."

Rather than re-litigate the decision, my attorney tried to reason with Justice Reynolds.

"The County Probation Department has recommended a sentence of probation," my attorney told the court. "I would ask you to agree, Judge Reynolds. Mrs. Crowe is a mother of three with no prior record of criminal activity. She has already served thirteen days. Throwing her back in jail would only punish her children. I don't think incarcerating Ms. Crowe will serve any additional interest of justice," he said.

Prior to my trial, the appeals attorney offered invaluable advice that challenged my criminal defense attorney's belief that I should never be put on the stand as a witness.

"I would like to speak on my own behalf," I said, looking directly at my attorney. On the advice of the appeals attorney, I had planned my thoughts on paper so I would be prepared. I was ready.

"I think that's a bad idea," my attorney said.

"I don't care," I told him defiantly. My freedom was on the line. I had no other choice. So, I briefly addressed the court.

"I apologize for not understanding the law. I had no intention of breaking any laws and certainly no intention of wasting the time and money of the court system," I said.

Now, it was the judge's turn to address the court. I held my breath as he spoke.

"To have this case in Willowbrook County Court, I must say, is exceedingly unusual, and I have struggled with all of this," he admitted. He called the ADA's argument reasoned and reasonable.

"Before I heard remorse today, I will tell you, I was thinking of a longer term of incarceration," the judge said. "Based on the facts that I heard at trial, based upon the pre-sentence investigation, it is the sentence of this court that you are hereby sentenced to four months in the Willowbrook County Jail with credit for time served," he said. The sentence also included a probationary supervision period of five years. I was crushed.

Court officers took me to a cell in the rear of the court, where I had gone the first time I was sentenced. This time, instead of crying, I chatted with the officers, who were very supportive.

"You need to file charges against your ex-husband," one of them suggested.

Their support felt good, even though, once more, they would be escorting me to Willowbrook County Jail.

Chapter Nine

RESILIENCE

"Out of difficulties grow miracles."

~Jean de La Bruyère

TUESDAY, JULY 26th

Once more, I found myself lying on a hard jail bed, the tarp-covered pillow crackling under my head. There was no "get out of jail" card here—that was clear. This journey was a game that no sane person would choose to play—the consequences were too weighty.

I felt numb as I faced what was to come. The difference this time was that I had embraced my situation with a heart that had surrendered to a greater power. Deep down inside, I knew that everything would work out. I just didn't know how or when.

"Miracles are real," I whispered to the walls of cell 220, my new home for the next little while. This time, I was in the upstairs facility since I was not considered a suicide threat. I felt a little happier here for some reason.

Of course, there were moments when I wanted to scream and rail at the unjust system that was trying to punish me for asserting my innocence and defending my rights. Why was I in jail while Darius was enjoying the summer at the lake, laughing with his friends? He admitted to committing the same "crime" I was accused of committing. Plus, he abandoned his family, stole everything from us, and was fighting tooth and nail to avoid paying support. In moments of intense emotion, I couldn't wrap my head around the injustice of it all.

But simultaneously, amidst the continuing madness, a transcendent peace kept me calm, and continuous prayer protected me from giving in to despair. I had a growing sense that if I stood firm and stared adversity in the eye, I had the opportunity for a level of personal growth that would have been impossible without this insane turn of events.

For several hours that morning, I sat on my bunk listening to a maintenance crew bang, banging on pipes or God knows what. The noise made it hard to think about anything other than the sound, which was a blessing in disguise.

After lunch that day, I was reading "The Zahir" by Paulo Coelho when suddenly, my new cell neighbor, a woman that was convicted of raping a twelve-year-old, approached me.

"So, tell me, Cinderella. It appears to me that you think you're all that," she said, her tone and expression like that of a fifteen-year-old mean girl. She took a step forward and asked, "I bet you think you're perfect, don't you?"

"What are you talking about?" I asked, confused, and, since I'm being honest here, I was annoyed. I had pretty much kept to myself since returning to jail. As far as I knew, I had done nothing to provoke her, so I had no idea why I was suddenly her target.

"Your arms are not proportionate to your body. Were you fat before?" she asked, pointing at my arm. "What nationality are you? And how the heck are your teeth so white?"

Then, she went on a rampage of questions, firing shot after shot, each one hitting me straight on. I sensed that she was testing me, but testing me for what? What was she trying to do?

I reached for the peanut butter sandwich I had saved for an afternoon snack and started grabbing quick bites to keep myself focused. It was imperative that I didn't let her entice me into an argumentative exchange. When she finally gave up on creating a scene, I noticed her standing near my cell with another inmate, the two of them whispering and looking in my direction.

Uh-oh, what are they up to? I thought, my senses suddenly on full alert. I had seen enough episodes of the TV series "Orange is the New Black" to know inmates often frame other inmates. By planting illegal stuff in their cells, the targeted inmate would receive additional time inside.

I would need to stay on guard.

WEDNESDAY, JULY 27th

It had been five whole years since Darius left us. While he was off enjoying his career and his new wife, I was sitting in jail, serving a sentence for a "crime" I didn't commit.

My emotions ran from feeling that my heart was broken to knowing that with each passing day, I was regaining my strength and growing even stronger. I finished The Zahir, which, even though I was literally locked up, made me feel free.

The story of Zahir helped me stay focused on the understanding that we have choices in life. One of the biggest and most important decisions we face is whether to hold on to bitterness caused by adverse events or to choose to live with a positive outlook and notice the beauty right where we are. The more I learned about myself, the happier I became. Feeling better about myself fueled my focus on rebuilding my life and creating something even more beautiful than what my old life had appeared to be.

As I started to feel better, my focus moved away from the inmates who enjoyed tearing others down to those who were genuinely concerned and helpful.

It was then that a woman who was facing drug charges offered me some valuable legal advice.

"Maria, you should check out the statute of limitations on insurance check fraud. You can't trust the system to be forthright about anything. You need to look it up for yourself," she offered.

Then, she suggested obtaining two copies of the check that Darius cashed without my signature.

She added, "You really need to file a sheriff's report and a civil suit. It sounds to me like you got shafted."

"I would say shafted is too nice a word. Let's face it—I got fucked over," I said. "Thank you so much for your help. You have no idea how much I appreciate this."

She offered more advice on appealing the criminal conviction.

"What is your attorney's plan for arguing?" she asked, a curious expression lifting her eyebrows.

I blinked. Her question surprised me, and my reaction was almost as if I was slapped back into the moment. I had no idea what my attorney was planning on arguing. It had never occurred to me to ask him, and he hadn't discussed it with me.

"You need to get clear on what he's going to do. You are paying him, after all. Sometimes lawyers forget that they report to you—not the other way around," she said.

I couldn't sleep that night thinking about our conversation. This entire situation was insane. Why did a random inmate seem to know more about the law than the last three attorneys I had hired combined? Why was I learning this from her and not my attorneys?

The next day, I sat down and wrote to my criminal defense attorney, my family court attorney, and my appeals attorney. It was time for me to assert myself. If these three lawyers didn't know as much as an inmate, it was obvious I would need to find someone else.

A few days later, I heard an officer shouting.

"MARIA, YOU'VE GOT MAIL!"

I happily snatched the Amazon box, which contained an array of items my dear friend had sent me as a gift.

"What did you get?" an inmate asked, looking over my shoulder.

Lifting the contents one by one, I said, *The Girl on a Train,* by Paul Hawkins, a puzzle book, oh, and look at this!" I said, holding the coloring book up with a laugh.

"Calm the Fuck Down," she read, giggling. "What a great title! Can I see it?"

"Sure," I said, handing it to her.

That night after dinner, while everyone sat around chatting, I couldn't stop thinking of my daughter's face on the day I left home for sentencing. I will never forget her eyes. She looked terrified when I told them I wasn't sure if I would be coming back. She clung to me, crying and repeating my name over and over. My heart broke every time she said the word.

"Mom. Mom. Mom," she cried.

I had tried to be strong, but seeing her like that, the dam holding back my own emotions broke. Tears poured down my face, mingling with hers, as I struggled to find words.

I didn't want my kids to lose faith in me. I would always be their mom, and I would do everything in my power to come home. I wanted them to believe in a fair justice system—one where an innocent person, a mom, is allowed to go home to her kids. There was too much to say, but I couldn't find the words.

As an inmate and a corrections officer tried to console me, the tears refused to stop. Honestly, I didn't even want them to. My heart was breaking.

THURSDAY, JULY 28th

I found out that my dog, a Poodle named Pantufa, bit my friend's neighbor, causing a gash in his lip that required 17 stitches.

"What the heck happened?" I asked my friend, who told me about the incident during a visit.

"Apparently, my neighbor went inside the house to use the bathroom. When Pantufa barked and growled, the guy, who was drunk at the time, stuck his face close to the dog cage, and Pantufa nipped him," he said.

"What the heck?" I said, my tone filled with confusion that had flooded my body as he was relating the story. I was suddenly terrified that the guy was going to sue me. Of course, I wasn't there, but the system already had me pegged as a criminal for something I didn't do. Would they hold me responsible for the bite anyway?

"There were puddles of blood on the kitchen floor. Pantufa bit him hard," he said, adding to my mounting anxiety. He must have noticed the change in my energy because he quickly said, "Oh, gosh, Maria, I'm sorry. I didn't mean to stress you out. It's all good. He said it was his own fault, so you don't need to give it any thought at all. It's taken care of."

I was instantly relieved. "Thank God," I said as a whoosh of relief replaced the anxiety. "Generally, Pantufa is so friendly. It's not like her to become so protective," I said.

Even poor Pantufa is stressed out, I thought.

"MAIL," shouted an officer. "MARIA."

She handed me a large manila envelope, the address written in Darius's hand. My fingers shook as I tore open the envelope, which contained four envelopes— one from each of my kids and one from Darius.

I tore open the first envelope, my fingers trembling.

The first letter was from Charlena, my youngest. Tears filled my eyes as I studied the picture inside. It was a colorful drawing of flowers and a big yellow sun. Putting it on the mattress next to me, I began to read.

Hi Mom. It's Charlena. I miss you and you are always in my heart. I will never forget you because you are my mom, my one and only mom and no matter what happens, I will always love you no matter what. I still have your bracelet, and when you come out, I will not let you out of my sight because I care about you— you are the best. I will never ever let go. I will chain myself to the wall and hold onto you and never let go. I will have a talk with that judge, and I'm not afraid. I will do whatever it takes. I love you so much—1,000,000,000,000,000,000 times. Everything is going to be great, and it will be better when you get back. These are all the things that you are: super mom, strong, loving, beautiful, caring, amazing, super supportive, fearless, hardworking, fun, funny, best friend, mom, honest.

Love, Charlena

I wiped my tears with the back of my hand as I folded the letter and put it back in the decorated envelope. Reaching for the next one, I eagerly tore the envelope open and began to read.

Hi Mom,

I miss you and I love you!

The girls' first play was good but the sound quality was horrible. It was all muffled and loud and ew. Also mom, can I please bring my Xbox? Please. Camp was fun. My friend Jacob cheered me up. He is awesome. Well, bye, mom, love you and miss you. Bye.

Love, Benny

I couldn't help but giggle just a bit when I re-read the letter. He was so in love with that Xbox. He would probably keep it with him constantly if he could. Even the picture he included showed him sitting in front of the television with the controller in his hand. What a funny kid. God I missed them.

The third letter was from my oldest daughter, Marissa.

Mommy,

Benny, Charlena and I are doing okay but I miss you so much and I will visit you a lot. I hope you are doing okay at the place (hotel). I love you and miss you a lot.

Mommy, you are so awesome and brave. Stay tough. We love you so much. To the moon and back times 1000000000000000000000!

Love, Marissa.

The drawing she included was of a huge red heart.

I read the letters over and over. There was nothing I could do to make them feel better except work my hardest to get back home to them. I grabbed some toothpaste and dabbed the back of each picture then hung them over the bed. Each picture fueled my already burning desire to get justice and go home.

Then, I stared at the envelope with Darius's handwriting. I didn't want to open it. Honestly, I wanted to rip it into a million pieces, throw it on the floor, spit on it, and grind it into the cement. But instead, I opened the envelope slowly and started to read.

Maria, I hope you use this time to reflect on your current situation and come to understand it's no one's fault but your own. I don't say this to be cruel or to rub salt in a wound. If you can step back from things and see ALL the mistakes you've made along the way (not just misunderstanding the law), it could be a long way to improving your life in the future. I sincerely hope, in the interest of the children, that you take full advantage of whatever counseling services are available to you to help you become a more cooperative, upstanding, and honest person.

Thanks.

Darius

I literally began to see red as the blood rushed into my head.

ALL the mistakes I made? Me? What mistakes except for trusting him and trusting the system that I believed would bring me justice? And he had the gall to capitalize the word ALL. The guy was a certifiable narcissist.

It suddenly struck me full force how fucked in the head Darius was. He cheated on his wife and abandoned his three kids because he needed to "find himself." Then he pressed charges against his wife for something he admittedly did himself! And he was telling me that I needed counseling? What a joke.

I crumpled up the letter and tossed it forcefully away from me.

"Uh-oh," the guard said. "That doesn't look good. What happened."

"I can't believe this guy," I said after telling her what Darius had written. "He honestly believes that he's a good guy looking out for the welfare of the kids by getting their crazy mom out of the way. The guy is sick," I said, still feeling my heart pounding in my chest.

The guard picked up the crumpled ball of paper and handed it back to me.

"Look, honey. Don't throw that letter away. Save it. It may come in handy one day," she said.

I realized she might be right, so I took it from her and flattened the paper before placing it in my journal. I didn't want to see it again, but I would know where it was if needed. I closed my journal with a resounding thump and tucked it away.

That evening, we were unexpectedly treated to storytime. The corrections officer joked and shared stories from the past.

"Two inmates have killed themselves since I worked here. One hanged herself in her cell during lunch break. In case you're wondering, that's why everyone is required to come out of their cells at lunchtime," she said.

We were then told about another woman who had jumped from the upstairs floor. I often wondered about that possibility. From where I stood, anyone could jump from that spot unimpeded if they really wanted to kill or injure themselves.

"That's why inmates with the longest terms are typically held upstairs," the officer added.

SATURDAY, JULY 30th

I woke up feeling happy that day.

"Thank you, God, for this day," I prayed. It didn't even matter that the light coming through the small window in my cell looked gray and heavy.

Despite being in jail, I was feeling peaceful for the most part—my evolving attitude of looking for joy in every moment helped me discover fun. I even found myself laughing at the smallest things, something I hadn't done for a while.

I began to realize that I was no longer feeling like a victim. I was in this crummy situation because there was a reason for it, and the reason was slowly being revealed.

I wrote a notarized letter for the Sheriffs to put in my file. I thought long and hard about giving permission for my son to visit me. I had the feeling that Darius would not allow my friend to bring my son but would instead insist on bringing him in himself. The idea of Darius coming into the jail to visit made me sick. The guy was a monster, and if I never saw him again, it would be too soon.

"He needs to be accompanied by an adult, but never by his dad," I told the Sheriff. "Darius loves creating drama. I don't want that in my life anymore."

The Sheriff laughed when he responded, "He's in the wrong place if he wants to start shit. We will take care of him for you."

"Thank you. I appreciate that," I said with a smile. "My son can come with any other adult—just never with Darius."

"You got it," the Sheriff said.

SUNDAY, JULY 31st

Only forty days left!

Don't ask me how the sentence was reduced, but I was overjoyed. I had no idea how all of this worked, but when I received the news from the Sheriffs, who seemed to be the only ones on my side, I wanted to do the happy dance. Instead, I took a shower and cleaned my "room." I even mopped the floor, which was something we were allowed to do if we could complete it in the allowed period of time.

When I finished, I washed one of my T-shirts in the shower with shampoo. I hated the thought of wearing clothing that someone else had worn, so I was overjoyed when my clothing was clean and smelled good.

My favorite corrections officer was working that day, and she promised to make sure the letter I wrote was filed.

"Thank you. I appreciate your help so much," I said with a smile.

"It's not a problem, Maria," she said, returning a grin.

I was excited for a visit with my son. I wanted to look good, so an inmate twisted my hair into a fun braid.

"Thank you! It looks so cute!" I said, staring at my reflection and moving my head from side to side to get the full effect.

The proverbial shit hit the fan, though, when Darius showed up and refused to let my friend bring my son in to see me. The officer told me Darius was insisting that he escort him.

"He says he wants to see you," the officer said.

"Darius wants to see me?" I asked, shock raising the pitch of my voice.

I knew it! I thought. The guy has me thrown in jail on a trumped-up charge just so he wouldn't have to pay child support, and then he wants to visit me? What kind of sick person does that?

Darius stood his ground, and so did I. Sometime later, he left the jail without allowing my son to visit.

I see nothing has changed, I thought. It's still his way or the highway. Why would he think I would want anything to do with the person who had me thrown in jail?

I had been desperately looking forward to seeing my son, so I felt terrible about the way everything went down. I soothed myself by noting the especially busy visitors' day. The room was loud, and with everyone talking at once, it would have been difficult to hear his voice in the din.

Thankfully, at the time, I didn't know that Darius had lied to my son telling him, "Mom doesn't want to see you—she wants to see her friend—not you."

MONDAY, AUGUST 1st

Peanut M&M's have always been my favorite, and during the time I was stuck in jail, I savored them even more. The crunch of the peanuts and the sweetness of the chocolate made me so happy and thankful.

"You know what would make this perfect? A big glass of cold Coca-Cola," I said to my friend, who was smiling and crunching on chips.

That night, I had a bad nightmare. My kids were scared, and I heard one of my daughters crying. My heart pounded as I tried to see her in the dark, but I couldn't find her. The dream went on and on as I searched everywhere, finally finding her stuck behind a shed, her eyes red and swollen, her hair in knots.

I woke up drenched in sweat.

I missed my kids so much. I was still angry that Darius had come and then refused to let me see my son. It was so much worse knowing that my son was mad at me and even angrier at my friend due to Darius's lie.

I finished reading *The Girl in the Train* and moved on to *How to Forgive When You Can't* by Jim Dincalci. The words that hit me like a runaway train said, "...you will be able to know when you truly forgive when you think of the offender, and he moves cleanly through your mind without crashing or burning."

"Oh, my God, this is funny! Listen to this," I said, sharing the words I had just read.

The inmates who had become my friends laughed and said, "Yup, you need to keep working on that one!"

"To forgive is to set a prisoner free and discover that the prisoner was you," Dincalci writes. His words hit me as painfully true. Even though I was in jail and far away from him, I was not free of Darius. Forgiving him would be a powerful way out for both me and my kids.

The first step was to acknowledge and then let go of the negative thoughts about him that blasted through my mind multiple times each day. I knew that forgiveness comes in stages—the more self-awareness I gained, the easier it would be. It was important that I let go of the resentment and hate that permeated every thought of him, so I set myself a goal of working through it before I left the jail.

Reading the bible and focusing on the story of Job kept me going. I wanted Job's happy ending.

TUESDAY, AUGUST 2nd

Thirty-eight days to go!

Suddenly, time seemed to be speeding up. Since the sentencing, I had been incarcerated for thirteen days— the same number of days that I was initially held without bail in May. Doing time felt a tad easier this time, even though it was a longer stay.

I think I was taking it better for two reasons. First, I knew what I was facing and when I was getting out. The last time the judge tossed me in here, I had no idea what to expect or when I was leaving. Second, I realized that being in jail was a short-term detox from all the drama occurring outside the jail walls. I was literally safe from Darius.

Unfortunately, my kids were the ones paying the price. Deep down inside, though, I knew they were part of me, which meant they had inner strength. They would feel scared for a while, but kids bounce back. They would be OK.

I spoke to my son that day. He sounded excited, which made me smile. My gut told me that Darius was recording our conversation, so I was careful with my words.

"Hi, honey. It's so nice to hear your voice. I miss you so much," I said.

"I miss you, Mom," he said with a happy lilt in his voice. Then, he told me about camp and a trophy he had won. "Mom, can I send you a picture of the trophy?" he asked. I was so happy to hear how upbeat he sounded.

"Of course! I can't wait to see it!"

I told him that if the phone automatically disconnected after fifteen minutes, I would call him right back.

"Honey, there are no bars or chains or anything of that sort here," I said, hoping to allay any fears his young mind may have conjured up. I missed my little man so much and wanted him to know I was fine.

Don't you cry, I repeated over and over in my mind. This call is about him, not you.

"MARIA! MAIL!" a corrections officer shouted a little while later. She handed me a letter from a friend containing pictures from "The Candy Land Musical" that my kids had participated in. I could not stop staring at the pictures. They made me so sad but happy at the same time. They were doing okay. I was sad to have missed out but thankful for the letter and pictures.

"CLERGY! WHO WANTS CLERGY?" the CO shouted.

I immediately lined up.

An older gentleman with soft-looking gray hair and twinkling brown eyes spoke. His message was beautiful. He said, "Trust in God and Jesus and give yourself to Him." I couldn't help smiling. It was a great day, and I was feeling happy.

Before bed, I started reading *Eleven Minutes* by Paulo Coelho. I was restless, making it difficult to fall asleep, so I prayed until I finally dozed off.

WEDNESDAY, AUGUST 3rd

I finally had a Bible again. The book came as a gift from my Bible study group. It felt so good to hold it in my hands and feel the power of the words inside.

I played a lot of ping-pong that day. My partner was pretty good, so it was more fun than usual. There was something comforting about the rhythm of the back-and-forth. After a great set, I did some coloring before heading back to my cell.

The cement 12-foot by 4-foot cell looked bleak with its peeling paint, stainless steel sink, and toilet without a cover. I still couldn't get used to sitting on it—it was always so cold. Just like in my old cell, a small plastic mirror hung over the dingy sink.

Sixty-five dollars remained in my account from my first jail stay, so I bought stamps, envelopes, and a birthday card for my middle daughter, whose birthday was in August.

I called my kids that day and talked with my girls.

"The Sheriff says I'll be coming home on September 9th," I said, laughing at their excited response. "In the meantime, you can visit every Wednesday and Sunday. I can't wait to see you. I miss you so, so, so much."

"How much?" my youngest daughter asked, bringing me back to the moment I stretched my arms out to demonstrate how much before wrapping them around her wriggling body.

"THIS much!" I said, once more laughing.

"Mom, can you come home earlier than September 9?" she asked.

"I can't honey. But it's only another four weeks. It's going to go by fast."

The focus of clergy time that day was forgiveness, the same topic I was concentrating on as I read "How to Forgive When You Can't."

A wave of gratitude almost brought me to tears, and I thought, it's amazing how God keeps sending me these wonderful messages.

"We cannot move forward unless we forgive," the Pastor said, his eyes earnest. The sincerity of his words hit me right in the heart. I couldn't go back and undo what happened, so I dug down to find forgiveness, or at least for some semblance of it, before I left jail.

Truthfully, I had not forgiven Darius at that point and wasn't sure I ever could. I was still harboring bad feelings that I was at a loss for understanding how to let go.

He treated me egregiously and with malicious intent, I thought, a feeling of anger rising. But the more I listened to the pastor speak, the more I realized how important it was to put it behind me.

Breathe deep, I thought. Focus on climbing Wright Peak when you get home.

Amidst the insanity of court battles with my ex, I found solace in nature. I took up hiking and had already conquered five of the Adirondack's forty-six peaks.

When I returned home, I planned to tackle every mountain in the range.

FRIDAY, AUGUST 5th

Getting outside early that day made me want to stay there. I found out that a family member had just passed away at forty-five years old, and I felt awful that I wasn't able to attend the funeral. One of the big insights that came from my jail stay is that life is very short. It's important to live it to the fullest.

I filed an application for disability relief, which I learned from the notary was usually done by the attorney at sentencing.

After spending one hundred thousand dollars the year before and nearly thirty thousand in the current year, it blew me away that I had to learn this from a notary. Why didn't my attorneys mention it?

"LOCK IN, LOCK IN, LOCK IN!" a corrections officer shouted as six officers charged into our space. Apparently, two of the inmates had gotten into a physical altercation, and one of the officers was accidentally hurt. Now, they were there to ensure a riot didn't break out.

Most of the inmates I met were convicted of crimes like DWIs, drugs, or violating probation. Sadly, many also suffered from mental illness. I learned more than I ever thought I would know about drugs and the illness they were intended to relieve.

For instance, I learned that Lithium, Effexer, (also known as Venlafaxine), Klonopin, Fentanyl, and other narcotics can cause death if they are taken together.

I learned that Effexor is an antidepressant that treats generalized anxiety, panic, and social anxiety disorders and that Klonopin can cause paranoid or suicidal ideation and impair memory, judgment, and coordination. Combining them with other substances, particularly alcohol, can slow breathing and lead to death.

You probably already know that Fentanyl is a high risk for addiction and dependence, but you may not know that it can cause respiratory distress and death when taken in high doses or combined with other substances, especially alcohol.

I had heard of Lithium and knew it is a psychiatric medication used to treat major depression or bipolar disorder.

Practically every woman I met in jail was taking one or more of the medications, and some were taking five different medications at the same time for psychological conditions such as depression, anxiety, bipolar, schizophrenic, and post-traumatic stress.

I couldn't help but think that the profit-driven pharmaceutical industry and the doctors who prescribe their products must know they are partially responsible for addictions and the resulting jail times that come as a result. These people are sick, and they need help.

Some of the women were incarcerated for eight to nine months or even one year. From what I learned there, drugs appeared at the root of a vicious cycle. Without being given the proper tools to help them recover and stay off drugs when they get out of jail, months later they were back.

One of the inmates shared a shocking story about her experience.

"I was never in trouble with the law until my doctor prescribed me Klonopin. He never warned me not to drink while using it. I ended up stealing a frickin' truck, and I have no recollection of any of it. The only thing I remember is waking up here," she said with a gloomy shrug.

Many of the women were suffering in ways I had never considered.

"Do you cut yourself?" I asked one woman when I noticed marks on her arms. She said nothing and walked away, hiding her arms.

Another woman told me that she took Lithium for bipolar disorder.

"It's fucking with my memory," she said.

"Why won't you get off the medication if you are losing your memory and maybe try a different medication?" I asked.

"My doctor won't take me off of it. He says without it, I'll go nuts," she said, her eyes sad.

A depressed woman I met had become addicted to heroin. It was her dream when she got out to use her experience by working in rehabilitation centers and helping other addicts recover. She explained a lot about why heroin is so bad.

"The ongoing depletion of dopamine levels in the brain makes it impossible for the user to feel much. They have a problem feeling pleasure or satisfaction from things that healthy people usually enjoy," she said.

When her husband, who appeared much older than her, visited, she looked so grateful when she said, "He saved my life."

That night, I was getting anxious. I filled up on Ramen and popcorn, hoping that a belly full of warm food would help me sleep.

SATURDAY, AUGUST 6th

I got into an argument with a woman who made a habit of creating drama. It started off as nothing.

"Could you please keep your voice down? I'm trying to hear this show," I said, feeling annoyed.

"No, I won't, bitch. I have a right to be as loud as I want," she said, the edge in her voice unmistakable.

Truthfully, I wanted to deck her. She was always causing trouble and talking behind everyone's back. But any mark against me at all would add days to my time. I needed to stay focused on getting home to my family. Plus, I had never hit anyone in my life and wasn't planning on starting now.

Later, though, when I confronted her, I was surprised at her response.

"I'm sorry. I usually am right, but I was wrong, and I'm sorry," she said.

"It's okay," I said, grateful that mending fences had been so easy.

"They were saying that someone like you would never talk to someone like me, so I assumed you were a bitch," she said.

One of the other inmates raised an eyebrow and said, "Wow, that was very out of character for her. I've never heard an apology from her."

My anxiety levels were skyrocketing over the process of appealing my sentence to a higher court. I concentrated hard on trying to control my thoughts. I spent time thinking about Pantufa and my cat Coco. I daydreamed about how great it would feel to get a massage, and I imagined myself having my hair and nails done as soon as I got home. The next month was going to feel like a year.

SUNDAY, AUGUST 7th

Thirty-two days left!

My son came for a visit! I love him so much. I held his hand the entire time. I felt bad, though, when I noticed a twitch in his right eye that happens when he's stressed.

Even though a psychologist there told me during a session that it was OK for children to see a parent cry, I refused to show my sadness. My kids didn't deserve that.

Falling asleep that night, I prayed the rosary while staring at their pictures. Each day was one step closer to getting back to them.

MONDAY, AUGUST 8th

Thirty-one more days until I'm outta here!

That day, we ate pancakes for breakfast, and for lunch, they served up coleslaw, which I don't like, and ham and cheese sandwiches. The ham looked as if it had been constructed from old pieces of ham that had been mushed together. Needless to say, I was hungry by dinner time.

It's hard for someone who has never been incarcerated to understand what it's like in jail. When friends talked about climbing mountains, going to the racetrack, and living life the way I used to, I was happy for them, but I felt left out.

Some of the inmates commented on the fact that I was no longer crying and talking about anguish all the time.

"It seems like you're feeling better this time around, Maria," one said.

"I am," I agreed. "I'm staying focused on the good in my life this time."

Focusing on forgiveness helped. I wasn't close to forgiving Darius for everything he had done, but when I felt myself getting angry, I was learning to redirect my thoughts. Maybe I had hit rock bottom for a reason. Without that experience, I wouldn't know and understand God in my life the way I was learning.

I finished "How to Forgive When You Can't" and moved on to "Veronika Decides to Die," by Paulo Coelho.

TUESDAY, AUGUST 9th

Thirty days left...

I was feeling a bit wistful and bitter.

Reflecting back, life had been good when I had a family and a successful career. Mine was the house where everyone loved to gather and hang out. I could only imagine since I lost everything and landed in jail, there wouldn't be anyone clamoring at my door.

I was doing everything in my power to forgive Darius. But what he had done was just plain evil. It was bad enough that he cheated. To lie about it and then leave his family and have his wife thrown in jail for the same thing he did was downright horrific. I missed my kids so much. I couldn't even write because my heart was in too much pain.

THURSDAY, AUGUST 11th

Twenty-eight days left!

"MARIA, ATTORNEY VISIT!" someone shouted.

"Are you sure?" I asked. I wasn't expecting a visit, but my appeals attorney was there to let me know he was requesting bail for me on Friday.

"I'm invested in this case, Maria. It's bullshit that you're in here," he said. "You'll probably need at least another four thousand dollars for bail. Do you think you can come up with that?"

I nodded my head. I would find a way.

"I submitted a notice of appeal. I can only control so much, but I will do my best," he said as he left.

I prayed so much that I think my brain went into overdrive because I woke up with a migraine. Sitting on my bed, I prayed.

"Please, God. You've got to help me figure this out."

The sheriffs and inmates agreed that it was impossible to get bail once you've been sentenced.

"He shouldn't be setting you up for another fall, Maria. You've already been screwed over too many times," one sheriff said, his expression serious. "None of us have ever seen anything like this before. Something's not right. Nobody pays bail twice."

Since I was locked up in jail, I had no way of checking. He was a professional, so I had no choice but to believe what he told me.

We went into another lockdown until 4 p.m. Sitting in my cell, I didn't want to get my hopes up even though I couldn't seem to control that either. I imagined myself home with the kids, walking along the river and feeling the sun on my shoulders.

That night, my prayer was simple.

"God, please help fix this mess."

FRIDAY, AUGUST 12th

Twenty-seven days left!

The vacation I planned with my kids would have started that day. Since my attorney's visit yesterday, I haven't stopped thinking about going home. He would be in Appellate Court at 10 AM fighting for my release.

"MARIA!" shouted the corrections officer on duty during lockdown, waking me from a snooze.

Excitement made me literally jump up from my bed. I'm getting out!

The officer's face was neutral. "Did you receive an inmate bracelet yet, Maria?" he asked.

Seriously? You woke me up for that? I thought as disappointment sucked the energy from my body.

I was trying hard to control my expectations, but my attorney's visit the day before had totally surprised me, and even more so when he said I could be leaving as soon as today.

If the hearing was at 10:00 AM, I would probably hear from him by 11:30 AM or noon. If I got approved, my friend promised to leave work, go to the bank, and speak with a bondsman. That would probably take until 2:30 PM. If all went well, I would be out of there by 4:00 PM or so.

Of course, this was all based on assumptions.

The day before, one of the women I was friendly with received good news when a friend of hers had sent a request for an early release form. She was so excited until she realized that she wasn't eligible because she was on probation. Her expression went from elation to sad so quickly that I felt bad.

"Fill it out and send it anyway," I encouraged. "You never know. Plus, remember what you told me yesterday about never putting what you don't want out in the universe? Be positive."

She laughed, but I could tell she was disappointed. While I waited to hear from my attorney, I knew I needed to temper my excitement and not set up an expectation of being home that night.

My attorney had explained the appeal process, so I knew it was a bit complicated and involved several steps.

First, he would file the Notice of Appeal, which must be filed within a specified time frame after the verdict or sentencing.

Second, I would have to pay for "paper," a record of the trial proceedings, including transcripts, exhibits, and rulings, which the appellate court would then review.

Third, with the gathered information, my attorney would prepare a briefing outlining his legal arguments and addressing relevant case law.

He told me that oral arguments would be an option but that he didn't feel he would need to present the case orally if it was well written.

Then we would wait for the Decision. The appellate court would review the trial record, briefs, and oral arguments to determine whether legal errors that warrant overturning the verdict or sentence occurred during the trial. The court would then affirm, reverse, or modify the lower court's decision.

All of this would cost me around five thousand dollars, plus the costs related to obtaining transcripts.

The argument would be that the court's decision to impose a jail term as part of the sentence was inappropriate. The focus once more would be that I had not forged anyone's signature or benefitted financially in any way. Plus, I had no prior criminal record, and my three young children needed me at home.

I was released on four thousand dollars bail, pending the appeal filed in Appellate Court.

I will never forget the experience of leaving jail that second time. The inmates and guards all stood up as my name was called. As I walked toward the enormous metal door that led to freedom, each inmate and officer either hugged me or gave me a high five, and everyone applauded. The only way to describe how I felt was triumphant.

"Kiddo, get out of here and good luck to you," one corrections officer said with a wide grin.

Since the day of my release fell during the one-week vacation I had long ago requested, it was my week with the kids, regardless of the parental schedule. I dialed quickly.

"Hi, baby! I'm coming to pick you up!" I said excitedly when my son picked up the phone.

Before my son could respond, Darius snagged the phone from him, his quick intake of breath revealing his shock when I exclaimed, "I'm out of jail and coming to get my kids."

"What are you talking about, Maria? You are in jail, locked up for a long time," he repeated over and over.

"Not anymore! I'm on my way to get my kids!"

While in jail, I had heard multiple horror stories of women trying to pick up their kids from an abuser. There were too many stories of women ending up back in jail when their abuser called the police on them. Armed with this information, I requested that a uniformed sheriff's deputy accompany me to Darius's house. When we pulled into the driveway, the kids came running out.

"Mom! You're here!" The team hug felt amazing. A song lyric ran through my head as little arms wrapped around my body.

"Reunited, and it feels so good!"

Darius had refused to let the kids pack their belongings, so the following morning, we returned, escorted by a deputy sheriff.

"Go on in and get what you need," I said. "We'll be right here waiting for you."

We had no money to go anywhere on vacation, so we spent the week at home. Thankfully, the house I was renting had a huge inground pool, so we swam and hung out, just enjoying each other's company.

With the appeal pending, I was presumed innocent under state law, so the probation part of the sentence ordered by the judge should have been suspended. However, in a shocking administrative error (for which no one has taken responsibility), I remained under probationary supervision for over a year and a half. It wasn't until the Appellate Court discovered the error that it was cleared up, but no one could give me my time back.

While on probation, I learned that it is like living only half-free. I met with my probation officer once or twice a week for more than eighteen months. I was prevented from leaving the state for any reason without approval, and requests to leave were not only expected to be submitted weeks in advance, but there was no guarantee of approval.

During the ordeal, my parents came for a visit from Cordova to stay in Massachusetts, which is just over the state line.

"You'll have to come here," I told my mom when she called to ask if I would be driving over to pick them up. She was confused when I explained why I couldn't meet her where she was.

"It's disgusting what he has done to you and the kids," she said. By now, my entire family had expressed their disappointment and sadness.

"I don't like to use the word 'hate,'" one family member said. "But it seems the only word that fits the situation. What an awful person he has turned out to be."

Every move I made was monitored. One day, when our dog escaped from our yard, the neighbors called animal control. Believe it or not, even that had to be reported to my probation officer.

I quickly learned that my probation officer was pretending to be my "bestie," inquiring about the kids and how I felt about local goings on.

"It's a pretty sneaky way of getting me to share information that could be used against me," I told my friend. "I wouldn't be surprised if he's buddies with Darius."

When all this was researched later, county prosecutors admitted that while word of the Appellate Court "stay" had reached the jail, forcing my release, "for reasons still unknown to the People, the stay was not communicated to the probation department, to this court, or apparently, to Ms. Crowe, who continued to appear for the supervision of the probation department."

The ADA defended himself, saying, "The People were not notified. But by saying that, I don't want to impute any impropriety. We didn't know about it."

I was incensed.

"Are you kidding me?" I whispered to my lawyer. "How could they not know about it? Doesn't anyone in this system talk to each other? Don't they have processes to ensure good communication?"

Eventually, the probation department applied to the court for an early discharge of my probation term, with the understanding that I had "served some year-and-a-half or so of probation, even though the papers may not reflect that..."

Oh, my God. Really?

My attorney formally requested that the judge discharge the remaining three and a half years of probation.

"The Supreme Court was unaware that Ms. Crowe was continuing probation visits after the stay. She should not have been on probation," the judge said. "Ms. Crowe will be released from probation. She has done well in satisfying the conditions," he further explained.

Then, I was told that the judge's decision required approval from the Appellate Court. They said I should not have been on probation during a pending appeal.

The bottom line is that I served thirteen days in jail the first time and another eighteen the second time before I was finally released on bail pending the appeal.

What a joke.

Chapter Ten

VICTORY

"The only limit to our realization of tomorrow will be our doubts of today."

Franklin D. Roosevelt

When I was released from jail in August, I was flat broke.

The probation department got right on my back, relentlessly pressing me to find a full-time position—now.

"Are you employed yet?" my probation officer asked at our first meeting.

"I'm working on it," I said.

"Well, you need to have a full-time job to meet your probation requirements. What about your previous place of employment?" she asked.

Since the arrest had destroyed my television career and reputation, I had very few options for finding work in my field. I contacted the construction company where I worked before my incarceration, hoping they had survived the financial strain they were suffering while I had been there previously. I hadn't even gotten paid for the last few weeks I worked, so they still owed me money.

"I called them. They're no longer in business," I said.

Panic was causing my skin to prickle. The court had ordered me to pay Darius "restitution" on half of the check that I had deposited (and used) for home repairs. I would need to come up with only a few dollars shy of one thousand dollars. Fear of not having the money in time fueled my already frenzied job search. And honestly, I was ordered to start paying while I was in jail—where I couldn't work. They started threatening that I would be in violation if I didn't pay.

"That money never belonged to him personally—it was to fix the house—the one he abandoned—along with his wife and his children—so that he could go fuck around," I ranted to my friend later that night. "I owe him nothing. He owes me. That was my money to use as I saw fit to fix the damned house, and that's what I did with it!"

My friend reached forward to pull me into a hug.

"Calm down, Maria," she said. "Karma's a bitch. He'll get his in the end."

"The end can't come soon enough for me," I said, succumbing to angry tears. "What about the checks he cashed without my signature? Why am I not getting half of those? This is all so infuriating that I feel like I can't even breathe."

"I hear you, and I can't even imagine what you're going through."

With the understanding that I would be going back to jail if I couldn't find a job and pay Darius back, I applied everywhere and even worked with the Labor Department to find something. Inevitably, though, there came a moment in each interview where I was asked the fateful question.

"Have you ever been convicted of a crime?"

I had no option but to be truthful. Lying would be another felony.

"Yes."

Each time, I held my breath, hoping the interviewer would show some sympathy and continue the interview. But each time, the interview ended there. I had to figure something out—and fast. I was a well-educated woman with great experience but the conviction prevented me from getting a job in my field.

One day, I noticed a "help wanted" advertisement for a company seeking home and office cleaners. I was simultaneously embarrassed and hopeful when I realized that the owner had been a "Family Matters" sponsor.

I swallowed my pride and dialed the number, my heart pounding and my fingers trembling. I was so embarrassed.

"I'm going through a bad divorce, and I need a job," I confessed to him. He bypassed the interview process and immediately brought me on staff.

"The job pays ten dollars an hour," he said matter-of-factly.

I would be cleaning kitchens and bathrooms, vacuuming, and mopping floors. It felt like a long, painful fall from being a television host and National Miss such a short time ago. Truthfully, taking the job didn't even make sense since I would have to pay a babysitter fifteen dollars an hour to watch my kids. But I had to have a job, or I would go to jail...again.

"I have no other choice, Rosa. The probation department has made it clear that I need to have a job or suffer the consequences."

The job started immediately. Since cleaning was not a cerebrally challenging job like I was used to, I created mini goals for the tedious tasks that made up my day. Doing so helped me keep my mind off Darius and the courts. But the circus continued.

The judge who had passed the order of protection request for me to Judge Greene more than four years earlier was assigned the custody decision.

The whole move struck me as another strategic step on Darius's part. If he had really wanted custody of the kids, wouldn't he have filed immediately rather than waiting four years?

It was always all about the money, I thought. Luckily, I used the anger that surged to scrub even harder at a stain on the bathroom floor. *I'll be the employee of the month for sure,* I thought as I moved my attention from the floor to the sink.

I remembered my struggle with a feeling of absolute terror that Darius would win. After all, he was a master manipulator with buddies in some high places, and to date, everything had gone in his favor.

On the day of the hearing, while the deputies transported me from jail into Family Court in handcuffs and chains, all I could think was, "I'm toast, so toast." But Judge Collins, the judge hearing my case kept glancing at me with a sympathetic expression. I wondered if she had remembered what happened four years earlier.

Thankfully, she delivered a decisive ruling.

"Petition denied. I will not grant Mr. Crowe legal custody of the children," she said, her brow furrowed as she looked over her glasses.

Days later, she recused herself from the case for a second time.

Later, for reasons I didn't understand then, Collins was thrown off the re-election ballot and replaced by Sarah Mathews.

In another interesting twist (as if there hadn't been countless twists already), Darius fired his lawyer shortly thereafter and hired Sarah to be his new attorney.

Our case was assigned to Judge Sinclair, who filled the vacancy left by Judge Greene. Judge Sinclair, too, had strong ties to the Willowbrook County establishment.

With Sinclair's appearance in the court, a change was suddenly made. Under Sinclair's ruling, Darius and I would share joint legal custody of the three children—with an important distinction: Darius gained final decision-making authority for our two daughters. At the same time, he assigned me the final decision-making authority for our son.

"The new terms supersede all prior court orders," Judge Sinclair announced.

As I stood scrubbing the sink in an office building bathroom, I could still picture myself standing in the court lobby, overwhelmed and distraught, a deluge of tears dampening the front of my jail clothing.

"I don't understand," I repeated several times. "How can this be? How is this *justice?* These are my *kids.*"

Darius's lawyer continued pressuring me to relinquish legal custody of my two daughters.

Darius admitted that he wasn't interested in taking custody of my son because he wasn't comfortable dealing with my son's ADHD. But for some reason, he was intent on getting the girls.

"He shouldn't have sole custody of any of them," I cried. "They're my babies. I birthed them. I raised them. I have loved them with my entire heart and soul every single day. I wasn't the one that abandoned them—he was. He only wants the girls so that he doesn't have to pay support for them. This is just about the money. It's disgusting. *He's* disgusting."

Then I looked at the law guardian and said to her, "How can you approve this? Why would you give an abuser control over two females? He doesn't have a vagina—he has a penis. He has no clue about raising girls."

I had a terrible feeling that this decision would be disastrous for us all. They used the threat of sending me back to jail as a weapon.

"You'll have no chance in court. You need to just turn them over and save everyone time. The judge is getting impatient," I was advised. "Keep in mind that you're a convicted felon."

I couldn't understand why my attorney was not acting as my advocate. Why wasn't she sticking up for me? I was angry and feeling powerless, but I couldn't just let him take my kids.

"I will not grant custody to that man," I said, my eyes red and my body stiff. "If he treats my girls like he has treated me, it could be bad for them. He's incapable of creating a healthy relationship with them. The man is a textbook narcissist."

I was infuriated and was having difficulty calming myself, so I was told that we would take a break.

"We'll reconvene after lunch," the judge said.

But after lunch, nothing was resolved.

Ultimately, I was forced to sign.

With a loud bang of the heavy gavel, the judge removed me from having any say on how my daughters would be raised. I wouldn't even have a say about emergency medical treatments or where they went to church.

His order of custody gave each of us first right of refusal whenever a child sitter was needed for more than four hours. We were also directed not to discuss our case with our media colleagues.

Not even five months later, Darius filed a petition with the court, accusing me of violating the order.

The judge's downgrade of my legal custody status came like an unexpected brick to the side of the head.

"He must feel pretty confident because he modified his petition to demand sole legal custody of all three kids. He's even asking for the removal of the right of first refusal provision," I told my new friend, Jackie.

I couldn't stop thinking about all the money I spent on attorneys. Each one seemed to know less than the other, and all of them were afraid to make any waves in the Willowbrook County system.

My mind wandered to the multiple women in jail who, shaking their heads in disbelief, had said, "You paid how much? And you're here? How is that possible? Have you ever thought about learning the law yourself? You know you have the right to represent yourself if you choose, right?"

Throughout the post-judgment disputes, I was blessed to meet people who shared similar experiences with the courts.

"This same thing happened to you, too?" I would ask each time. It seemed impossible that this had been happening for years right down the street from where we lived and worked. So many people were impacted by what felt to me like a totally unjust system.

"We're nothing to them. They're members of a club, and they watch out for each other. We are nothing more than collateral damage."

I was blessed that each and every one of these people offered me guidance and continued support. Their stories convinced me that I was just another statistic of the broken court system.

As Jackie and I began to realize how similar our stories were, Jackie, also a mother of three, and I became fast friends. The closer we became, the more of her story she shared.

"My case started in 2005. Think about what a waste of taxpayer money it is to be still grinding through the court system all this time. It's been ten years! And that's just me. What about all the other people stuck in the system? I can't even imagine spending so much money on so much b.s. That money could be spent to do good in this county." She shook her head in disgust.

She, too, had challenged parts of a divorce judgment ordered by Justice Greene.

"Because I earned a decent salary working for General Electric, I was saddled with the lion's share of the family debt, and Judge Greene gave me zilch for child support. You know from experience how expensive it is to raise three kids. How was I supposed to get along on what Greene decided was sufficient?"

"I had the same experience! Darius was making close to one hundred fifty thousand dollars a year, and I was awarded seven hundred seventy-five dollars. All I can think is Judge Greene got screwed over on child support at some point, so he is taking it out on any woman who dares stand up for more," I said.

In Jackie's case, the New York Appellate Division found that the Supreme Court erred in its divorce judgment as well as two post-judgment orders. It returned the case to the Supreme Court recalculations in child support and maintenance.

Five years later, Jackie was still waiting for the 4th Judicial District to do its job and enforce the higher court's amendments.

"Fifteen years," Jackie said. "During that period of time, there were six judge recusals and more than one hundred twenty-five court appearances."

"When did you have time to work with that many court appearances?" I asked, shocked.

Her laugh was wry. "It's not like I had a choice. Thankfully, my boss backed me up, or it would have been difficult."

As time went on, I learned that her ex-husband ignored the court orders and refused to pay more than one hundred thirty thousand in child support. Yet Jackie was the one who was facing jail time for not signing over to her ex-husband most of the proceeds from an insurance settlement check.

Getting to know Jackie was an incredible stroke of luck. The more we talked, the more I learned.

"I wish I had met you five years earlier, Jackie. This whole experience may have been a lot easier if I had your insights earlier."

"Possibly," she said. "But it still wouldn't have been easy. This is all so wrong, and no one is pushing back on the system."

Through my relationship with Jackie, I learned about the close ties between judges, attorneys, and others in county political circles. The more I learned, the more I understood the clannish nature of the legal system. Suddenly, everything made so much more sense. No wonder Darius had so easily been able to manipulate his position. As a well-known State Police media representative, he was in the club.

As we plotted our next moves, I decided to represent myself. One night, as we chatted, I said, "Jackie, I'm firing my lawyer, and I'm going to represent myself. No one knows my story better than I do. I'm smart, I'm a great researcher, and I aced my political debate class. I've got this from here on."

I needed to be as big as I was and stand up using my own voice. So many of the lawyers were just plain useless, and all they worried about was getting paid.

"I think you need to ask yourself why Darius keeps hiring lawyers with connections. Once you understand the strategy, you can outsmart him," Jackie said.

The more I understood Jackie's case, the more I was blown away by how close her circumstances were to mine. She, too, was being threatened, and I guessed it was because she wasn't afraid to question the judge's decisions. She had no problem going over their heads to the higher courts to appeal any unfair rulings.

"Now that they are being held accountable, they are freaking out," she said. "They'll try to scare you, Maria, but don't let them—those of us who have been treated like this need to stand together. The system needs to be held accountable for unjust treatment."

After everything that happened to me, I have had a lot of time to think about all of this. Personally, I think the problem is that our society holds judges in very high esteem. They aren't questioned in our culture, which makes them somehow untouchable. Plus, in New York State, they are extremely well compensated with salaries of over two hundred thousand.

Another big issue is the length of their terms. They establish deep footholds because, while U.S. representatives serve from two to six years, Family Court judges are elected to 10-year terms.

This next point may be more than you're interested in knowing, but I think it's important to note. Did you know that local political party leaders appoint judges through a judicial nominating commission, and governors, mayors, or county executives can appoint judges to fill unfinished terms? The systems are tightly interwoven.

"Emily Collins found this all out the hard way," Jackie said. "While she was an incumbent Family Court Judge Republican Committee, the county turned its back on her and endorsed someone else for the position!"

"Ouch," I said. "That's horrible. Emily was the judge who came through for me by denying Darius's petition for sole custody of the kids. But then, only a few days later, she recused herself from the case. I was so confused by that move."

"I'm not surprised," Jackie said, shaking her head. "Did you know that the GOP inexplicably endorsed an attorney named Sarah Mathews over Emily Collins?"

"Sarah Matthews? Really? I didn't know that!" I said. "Darius hired Sarah as his attorney."

"Why am I not surprised?" Jackie asked, raising an eyebrow. "Emily alleged an unfair and rigged nominating process set up by the Republican Party. They wanted to ensure that Mathews got the endorsement. Emily said she was denied access to contact information for local town committee members that Sarah received because she was a neighbor and friend of the county Republican chairman," Jackie said.

"Wow. This makes so much more sense than it did before. No wonder everything is so screwed up," I said, feeling even more incredulous than I already did.

"Yup, and when Emily Collins announced that she would run against Mathews in a primary for Family Court judge, the county Board of Elections removed her from the June Republican ballot. The board ruled that she didn't have enough signatures to qualify for a spot on the ballot. So, Sarah got herself elected."

"This is all sicker than I realized," I said. "How does anyone get a fair trial in this county?"

"You just have to know the right people," Jackie quipped. "Emily's campaign manager told the press that by exploiting the election procedure to remove her opponent (Emily), Sarah was showing us that self-serving politics outweighs balanced judgment."

Not long after that conversation, Darius filed yet another petition. This time, he asked the Judge to reduce his monthly child support payments. He claimed that he was being forced to resign from his job with the State Police.

I was suspicious as hell. "Really? Where's the proof?" I asked.

In case you don't know how this works, when it comes to child support, trial courts calculate a parent's gross income by examining their most recent tax return and taking into consideration past employment experience and future earning potential. If Darius voluntarily quit his job, he would not be entitled to pay less for child support.

I moved to dismiss Darius's latest petition and prepared myself for another court showdown, once again in front of Magistrate Blake.

This time, though, I would be using a new strategy. It was time for me to reclaim my voice. I had received so much advice from inmates, friends, and an extremely credible "inside source" from Willowbrook County Family Court. I dropped most of the attorneys handling the case and hired Laura Thompson, who had the reputation of a shark. She was the first and only attorney who read through all the court orders to learn everything about the case. She would handle the cases in the appellate division.

"It feels so good to have someone who is actually going to fight for me," I told Jackie.

It was an excellent decision to hire her, but still, after a lot of reflection and consideration, I decided it was time for me to represent myself on the support issue. I was tired of paying lawyers who were afraid of getting on the bad side of judges or who were nervous about going to trial. It was time for me to stand up for myself. I had been playing small for far too long.

If nothing else, being incarcerated taught me that I needed to own my voice. So far, nobody knew my side of the story. Not one of my attorneys had stood up for me. They had all been too afraid to speak up. In hindsight, I should have pushed back against them and spoken up for myself.

I started researching on my own behalf. I needed to understand who, if anyone, had jurisdiction over the state and county court systems. It was then that I discovered Chief Judge of the Court of Appeals Diana Russo.

A month after Darius filed his latest petition, I wrote to the chief judge to ask her to investigate the underhandedness in Willowbrook County Supreme and Family courts. In my letter, I told her that I had been waiting for nearly a year for Magistrate Blake to address the petition, but he kept rescheduling and adjourning court dates.

"According to the Administrative Rules of the Unified Court System & Uniform Rules of the Trial Courts, sect 205.43," I wrote, "the willful violation or enforcement of an order of support shall be scheduled as soon as possible for a first appearance date in Family Court, but in no event more than 30 days of the filing of the violation or enforcement petition. The hearing must be concluded within 60 days."

Based on the scuttlebutt I heard from sympathetic court employees, I believe my letter to the chief judge had a real effect. Things finally started moving.

To prepare for trial, I put my entire heart and full faith in the hands of the Lord as I trained myself as a trial attorney. I studied for weeks at the Law Library in Willowbrook, immersed in piles of red and black volumes containing thousands of pages.

At first, the books meant nothing. I had never opened a law volume. To me, they were all numbers and names written in legalese. I remember sinking my face into my hands and praying for the openness I needed to understand them. It took some time, but finally, I began to get it.

I collected checks and receipts for expenses I had incurred over the years. Obtaining evidence from Darius wasn't nearly as difficult once I learned the power of serving subpoenas. By writing my own subpoena documents, I was able to acquire Darius's salary, retirement accounts, employment situation, and pretty much anything else I needed.

I practiced for trial by preparing a case that focused on evidence. It was imperative that I show the court the amount of child support that I was entitled to under the law, support my argument with case law, and present the evidence calmly.

I meticulously prepared numbered documents, exhibits, and index cards with prepared questions and law quotes from the library. Key words like "objection" had to come automatically, so I practiced and then practiced some more.

On the day of the trial, I sat in the courthouse's waiting area, feeling levels of anxiety that matched those of the period when my career crashed and burned. I surveyed the area, working hard not to show my anxiety. Then I saw her—Darius's lawyer.

I prayed harder than I ever had before.

"Holy Spirit, please speak through me," I asked. Then, I reminded myself that the truth always wins. "You have nothing to hide, Maria," I whispered.

About fifteen minutes later, she walked up to me, looked me straight in the eye, and smiled.

"I have great news for you," she said. "My client is asking if you want to settle to avoid trial. He will continue paying the same, and we can just tell the judge that we settled. There's no need for a trial."

The implication of the suggestion changed something in me, and a feeling of total peace settled in my body and mind. Darius hadn't agreed to anything in years. The man put me in jail. After everything that had gone down, did he really think I would settle?

"Absolutely not," I told her, my tone confident and unwavering. "We are going to trial."

I had the sense that when an opposing party in a legal dispute, one that has fought me tooth-and-nail for years, suddenly offers to settle, he must have a sense that he is going to lose.

We were called into the courtroom.

"Ms. Crowe has informed me that she will not settle," Darius's lawyer said in an accusatory tone.

Magistrate Blake turned his gaze to me, and we locked eyes.

"Is this true, Ms. Crowe?"

"It is, your Honor. I want the trial to start now."

I presented several exhibits and information obtained through subpoenas. The material demonstrated that Darius had presented false and inconsistent financial disclosures.

"You can see here, your Honor, that Mr. Crowe was making an obvious attempt to lessen his child support payments by submitting incorrect financial disclosures," I said, feeling triumphant.

Following the trial, Blake finally ruled on support petitions filed months earlier. While he dismissed my petition, Blake also dismissed Darius's and forced him to continue to pay the child support amount of $1,718 through the Support Collection Unit as well as eighty-three percent of any unreimbursed medical expenses.

In his decision, Blake agreed that Darius had not demonstrated sufficient changes of circumstances to warrant a recalculation of child support. In fact, Blake said, Darius was earning more than one hundred twenty-two thousand a year while his new wife was making eighty-three thousand.

The magistrate also ordered Darius to pay more than $2,900 in arrears. In the order, Blake wrote that Darius had been lucky all these years because the amount of child support that he had paid significantly deviated from the law's calculations.

What I took away from this pivotal moment was that, by removing the emotion and presenting a supportive case based on facts, the law was on my side.

What an amazing victory! I thanked God for His love and strength. With patience, persistence, passion, and prayer, together, we conquered Darius's team of lawyers and held on to what was fair.

Chapter Eleven

TRIUMPH

"The greatest glory in living lies not in never falling, but in rising every time we fall."

Nelson Mandela

Stung by not winning a reduction in child support, Darius filed a petition accusing me of violating Family Court Judge Sinclair's order that awarded Darius final decision-making authority for our girls.

Destroying my career and then having me put in jail (for doing the exact same thing that he did) didn't seem to be enough for Darius. It seemed clear to me that his loss in front of Magistrate Blake threw him for a loop, and he was trying to regain control. Otherwise, why would he continue to come after me? What threat was I to him?

At that point, Darius decided to modify his court petition to demand sole legal custody of all three children. We went to trial to contest not only his petition for sole legal custody but also my attempt to obtain Darius's eighty-three percent share of a nearly five-thousand-dollar orthodontist bill. I had paid the balance in full and was asking him to pay the share stated in the court order.

When I was a kid, I was taught that judges are fair, impartial, and thoughtful. When considering cases, we could count on them to weigh the evidence and make their rulings based on that evidence. However, in the case of Judge Sinclair, I got the distinct impression that fairness was not one of his strong suits.

His favoritism seemed blatant in a family court appearance when Darius showed up without an attorney. Judge Sinclair kept giving him counsel from the bench.

"You should file an amended petition, Mr. Crowe," Judge Sinclair told Darius. "Ms. Thompson is a very experienced attorney. It would be a good idea for you to retain counsel."

Then Sinclair went on to say, "Again, I think you want to seriously consider counsel. On your petition, you should state cause of action and attach exhibits."

The trial started shortly afterward, with Judge Sinclair presiding. At the start, Darius appeared without an attorney.

Appealing to Judge Sinclair's sympathy, Darius said, "My ex-wife has been combative since the beginning, and the conflict has continued for over seven years now."

Laura Thompson, on the other hand, was fully prepared with all the necessary facts, figures, and dates.

"Objection," she interrupted. "Mr. Crowe has filed over half of all petitions over the last seven years. Many of those petitions were vindictive and harmful toward my client," she said.

Darius brought no evidence and showed no justification for awarding himself sole legal custody of the kids.

"I believe Darius loves our kids," I said. "But the truth is that Darius has always put Darius first—

sometimes at the expense of the children. I am the parent who takes them to doctor appointments and sports practices. Plus, it's me who helps them with their homework," I said.

With Darius launching a new custody battle, I amended my own petition to seek sole legal and physical custody of the children.

"This is good," Jackie said when she read over the petition I had prepared. "It's great that you have so much detail here."

My petition was straightforward. I included times and dates for instances in which Darius had refused to work cooperatively on decisions regarding the kids. I cited one specific parenting conflict involving one of them, noting his inability (or unwillingness) to discuss a school safety issue.

"Thanks. I'm learning detail is super important. I have a journal where I've been keeping track, so I think it's detailed enough, right?" I asked.

"Absolutely," she said. "Unless..."

"Unless what?" I asked.

"Were there any medical decisions that he pushed back on?"

"Good point," I answered, grabbing my calendar, which included detailed notes. "There were several."

"Include them," she said.

Darius filed a pro se motion to dismiss my amended petition, and he represented himself during the first three days of the trial. When he finally hired an attorney, it was a partner at the television station where he was often interviewed who was a friend of Judge Sinclair.

"You've got to hand it to him. He knows how to use his connections," I told Laura.

At the time, Darius was mopping up a huge salary and making extra money doing additional gigs. I, on the other hand, was mopping floors and cleaning toilets for ten dollars per hour.

Early that same year, I realized I had no choice but to file for bankruptcy. I was literally drowning in legal fees, which made it difficult to breathe. I will admit that it was not one of my prouder moments, but I felt I no longer had a choice. With my reputation and career ruined, I would have had to work for the rest of my life to pay back even half of the debt owed. To make matters worse, I knew that declaring bankruptcy would damage my credit.

"I was convicted and have done jail time, and now I'm declaring bankruptcy. It's not exactly the dream life I saw for myself," I told Jackie with a sigh. "However, when I considered the pros and cons, I felt like I had no other choice."

"You're doing the right thing, Maria. The stress of shouldering all of this would kill most people. And here you are smiling," Jackie said.

"Barely," I answered with a laugh. "At one point, I couldn't even afford toilet paper and food for the kids. But I kept the faith then, and I will continue to do the same now."

At the third custody trial date, the judge acknowledged updates in the case, including my amended petition seeking sole legal custody based on a change of circumstances.

"Discussions today will be explicitly limited to the alleged violations of the order of custody and parenting time," Judge Sinclair said. "Be assured that I will conduct a hearing on Ms. Crowe's petition for sole legal custody upon the conclusion of the violation proceeding."

When the proceedings ended, the petition was not discussed.

That August, though, Magistrate Blake presided over a separate trial involving Darius and me regarding a petition that I had filed nearly a year earlier. In it, I alleged his failure to pay a child support order and medical expenses for one of the kids.

Blake decided that Darius "unknowingly" failed to pay one thousand nine hundred sixty-two dollars in child support. He was instructed to pay it within two weeks through the Child Collection Unit. It was also decided that Darius owed five thousand thirty-one dollars in health-related expenses. Finally, a decision was made in my favor!

Then came the greatest legal victory of all.

"Hi, Maria. I've got some really good news," Laura Thompson said, excitement flooding her voice. "The order for jail time has been overturned!"

"What?" I asked, afraid to believe what I was hearing. The threat had been hanging over my head for so long that I could barely believe this turn of events was true. "So, you're saying I don't have to worry about going back to jail?"

"No, you don't. The decision says that 'in the interest of justice,' time served wraps it up."

The long and expensive journey to remove the ongoing and anxiety-inducing threat of returning to jail came on the heels of the support win. The jail sentence handed down by the Willowbrook County Supreme Court two years earlier was being overturned by the Appellate Court.

"Oh, my God! And I do mean, thank you, God! This is amazing. Laura, I can't thank you enough!" The excitement and relief mixed so abruptly that another flood of tears rose. I couldn't believe it! I would not be returning to jail! My faith and unrelenting determination (and money) had paid off.

"I'll read you part of the Appellate Court's decision," she said.

"Okay," I said, another flood of excitement making my heart race.

"It says, 'Ordinarily, we refrain from exercising our power to modify a sentence, unless the sentencing court abused its discretion, or extraordinary circumstances warrant such a modification. In our view, the circumstances surrounding the commission of the crime and the defendant herself are extraordinary and warrant exercising that power. The judgment is modified, as a matter of discretion in the interest of justice, by reducing the jail sentence imposed to a term of time served.'"

"I don't even know what to say, Laura. I'm so excited! I knew this would happen at some point, but I'm so excited that it happened now!" I said.

A few weeks later, I returned to Willowbrook County Supreme Court feeling triumphant.

"Be careful not to look too confident," my attorney warned in a whisper. "You need to appear humble."

As I stood before Judge Reynolds, he said, "Please state your name for the record."

All I wanted was an apology or at least some acknowledgment that he had made a mistake. Instead, he noted that the court had received a decision, memorandum, and order from the Appellate Division that modified the judgment.

"I credit you with satisfying your five-year probationary period, Ms. Crowe. Your sentence has been changed to time served."

Then, he advised me that if I felt I had been subjected to any illegality or injustice, I should file a notice of appeal with the district attorney and county clerk within thirty days.

Illegality or injustice? What about the years of humiliation? How about going to jail for the same thing that my ex-husband had done when he received no repercussions? How about a case I witnessed where a local chef, after pleading guilty to second-degree grand larceny for stealing one hundred seventy-five thousand dollars from the restaurant he worked at, was given only five years of probation and no jail?

Memories of the events elicited mixed emotions. On one hand, I was ecstatic. I was finally putting the most shockingly painful episode of my life behind me. I was even a little proud of myself for having the gumption to confront the Fourth District.

At that exact moment, though, I felt confused.

Is this it? Am I supposed to just move on with my life after the criminal justice system has run roughshod over it for years? The damage has been done on so many levels. My old life is lost, and my reputation and career are ruined.

I shivered as I thought about the damage. I spent many months worrying about the kids and our finances and fighting for my freedom. Plus, I was dealing with fallout from the arrest. All of this wouldn't just cease to exist. I would suffer the ramifications maybe for my entire life.

To make matters worse, when I was arrested, the story was headline news.

"Local newscaster arrested on forgery charges!!!"

But the news cycles moved on, and both the press and the public forgot about my case. When I won the appeal, though, only a few news services even covered it—the ones that did published tiny little stories on the bottom of page ten.

Our local newspaper even portrayed Darius as a victim and referred to him as "a long-time State Police spokesperson."

But with the threat of jail no longer hanging over my head, I focused all my energy on reclaiming my parental rights, namely legal custody over my daughters. I faced an ongoing trial before Judge Sinclair only to suffer the same result.

"This is so infuriating, Jackie! Sinclair dismissed another of my petitions. Why has he acted on nearly every single one that Darius has filed, but he dismisses mine?" I asked.

"I would call it the 'good old boys club,'" she said. "It's so blatant, but for some reason, no one is willing to step up to point out the beast."

I agreed. These people called themselves men, but from what I could see, they were insecure children covering each other's backs even when they knew they were in the wrong.

"Sinclair says this last one fails to state a cause of action. On the previous petition, he said there was a paperwork technicality, and the one before that, which was an order of protection, he claimed did not constitute a family offense. I'm part of the family, so if I'm feeling threatened, how is that not constituting a family offense?" I asked.

I was shut down again when I submitted evidence of changes in the kids' and Darius's circumstances. Shortly thereafter, Sinclair threw out my request for legal custody without even conducting a hearing.

A parental incident in Darius's home became a court issue when my son called crying and asking for my help.

"Mom, Dad and Elara are abusing me. Can you come and get me? Please!"

I didn't ask a lot of questions. My son never asked for help, and he sounded scared. I jumped in my car and drove quickly to Darius's home, where I found him chasing my son down a very busy street. When I pulled up, my son hopped in the car and locked the door.

"Drive, Mom!" he said, tears running down his face.

Darius gave me a dark look and said in a threatening tone, "Jail wasn't enough for you, was it, Maria? You want more."

As I sped away, a shiver of cold fear ran through my body. Darius seemed to have the "justice" system on his side. This could get worse, but I was a mom. I had to help my son.

When it was time for the decision, Sinclair stated from the bench: "The court finds that the father's actions constitute appropriate parenting. In contrast, the mother's actions fly in the face of any reasonable attempt to co-parent."

Ugh.

Three months later, I launched a second modification proceeding for sole legal and physical custody. The grounds were Darius's failure to work cooperatively with me.

When the dentist said the kids desperately needed braces, Darius refused to pay. He petitioned the court, accusing me of violating the court order that gave him control over healthcare decisions. Darius predictably filed for dismissal.

Two months after that, Sinclair granted Darius's motion and dismissed my petition without conducting a hearing and without even allowing me to submit evidence.

After this dismissal, I realized I had no recourse but to go over Sinclair's head. I wrote a letter to Justice Santini, an administrative judge of the 4th Judicial District.

"I am tired of being discriminated against in Willowbrook County Family Court," I wrote in a letter that I copied to the New York State Unified Court System, the American Civil Liberties Union, and the New York State Attorney General's Office. "Mr. Crowe has filed seven petitions before Judge Sinclair, and all have been heard. A six-day custody trial was granted over frivolous matters, yet when I filed two petitions, one was immediately dismissed, and the other one dismissed with prejudice without a hearing."

Meanwhile, back in the family court system, "Lincoln Hearings" were being conducted. These allowed the kids to discuss their concerns and custodial preferences in confidence rather than forcing them to speak openly in front of their parents in a courtroom.

In a letter from an attorney for the children, Judge Sinclair was informed that based upon the evidence, the attorney was "not in support of the father's request granting him full legal custody of the three children...and should the court be inclined to modify legal custody, I would be in support of the mother having full legal custody of all three children."

Days later, Judge Sinclair released his decision and order.

"Full legal custody will remain with Mr. Crowe," he said.

"What? How is this fair and just?" I asked, barely able to believe what I was hearing. "All three kids have made it clear that they prefer to be with me!"

Sinclair answered, "Mrs. Crowe, you willfully violated the earlier court order, and you awarded Darius sole legal custody of all of the children, 'in order to hopefully limit the friction between the parties.'"

Once more, the system was working for Darius and against me and the kids.

By then, I understood the game, though. In the eyes of the judges, Darius was working as a State Police spokesperson. Since judges worry about any negative publicity, Darius blatantly used his position in the media to garner their support. During one of our hearings with Judge Sinclair, Darius even brought a friend who was the general manager of a local news outlet to court.

My attorney was extremely angry about the custody decision. We filed a notice to appeal and a motion requesting a stay pending the appeal. The attorney representing the children backed the motion.

"I'm so grateful that he's on my side," I told Jackie one night while we chatted.

"You are definitely blessed there, kiddo. Just keep staying positive. The good energy will pay off in the long run," she said.

I was becoming exhausted trying to find positives in this situation. On days when I was struggling, I reminded myself over and over that it was important that I trust that God had a plan. I knew He would give me the strength to deal with the decision. It wasn't fair, but I accepted it as part of my positivity training. My experience could help others at some point. So, I kept my eyes forward and tried not to look back.

Not two weeks after Sinclair's outlandish order, I received notification that the Unified Court System's 4th Judicial District had reassigned case action to Judge Sinclair, the very judge from whom I was seeking a stay!

The whole thing was a major conflict of interest, so I sat down to write to Justice Santini to urgently request a different judge.

"You can't assign the same judge I am asking a stay from," I told Santini.

My letter was ignored.

Unsurprisingly, Sinclair declined to rule against his own order and dismissed my motion for a stay, calling it defective.

Sinclair's decision to grant Darius full legal custody, despite the wishes of the kids, their attorney, and me, left me so enraged that I contacted several elected officials.

I wrote to the Chief Judge of the Court of Appeals and told her about the systematic problems and biases that I and other women had encountered in Willowbrook County courts.

I recounted my story in letters to New York's top elected officials, including the governor and two senators. (Both senators replied, saying the matter was out of their jurisdiction.)

I filed a discrimination complaint with the New York State Attorney General, explaining how the judges and district attorneys in Willowbrook County were abusing their power and needed to be stopped. The Civil Rights Bureau replied, saying it could not investigate the complaint because it did not appear to allege "a pattern or practice of discrimination."

The New York Civil Liberties District wrote back to me saying, "We are aware of the systematic abuse that exists in local courts throughout the state, not only in Willowbrook County, and one of our attorneys brought that knowledge to bear when carefully reviewing your complaint. Our organization has wrestled with how to attack this problem and we have not, as yet, devised what we think would be a winning strategy. Consequently, we cannot assist you in this matter."

How disappointing. They admitted to being aware of a problem, but their reasoning behind not helping out was that they hadn't devised a winning strategy. Were they working on a strategy, or were they, too, sitting back, aware of what was happening but unwilling to work on a solution?

I contacted the Unified Court System for copies of quarterly reports pertaining to petitions and motions filed in my case dating back to the beginning. I attached dates of appearances before judges Greene, Collins, Dubois, Blake, and Sinclair.

What I learned was pathetic. My case had been going on for eight years, and not one of the judges filed quarterly reports on it—in some cases, they didn't even file recusal letters!

There was only one way to go: up.

If I wanted to get my kids back, I would need to exercise my constitutional right to appeal Sinclair's decisions to a higher court. I needed an appeals attorney to represent me in the matter.

So, I hired Moneek Makbryd, the best appeals attorney in the capital city. She was great, extremely professional, and fought hard for me.

"You have been wronged, Maria. I want to make this right," she said, her expression earnest.

Appeals were filed with the Appellate Court, challenging Sinclair's legal child custody ruling. On appeal, the attorney for our children argued that the Family Court's award of sole legal custody to the father was an error.

Eight months later, the Appellate Court handed down a strongly worded decision on my appeal.

It was a sweeping victory!

The Appellate Court reversed three of the Family Court's orders. It remitted the matters to Willowbrook County Family Court for new hearings before a different judge within forty-five days.

"Sinclair's out!" I practically yelled with excitement into the phone.

"That's excellent!" Jackie laughed. "The tides are turning in your favor."

Pending the new hearings, the Appellate Court ruled that I would once again share legal custody with final decision-making authority over my son.

In stark language, the Appellate Court agreed with me that Judge Sinclair had acted improperly.

"Given the circumstances, timing, and nature of Family Court's improper factual findings, we cannot foreclose the possibility that Family Court prejudged the case or was predisposed to a certain outcome on the father's petition," the Appellate Court's decision stated.

"Moreover, by summarily dismissing the mother's petitions, Family Court created a situation in which only the father could pursue and obtain relief on allegations that the mother also raised."

The decision further stated, "Such factual findings and credibility assessments have no place in an order resolving a motion to dismiss for failure to state a claim."

In other words, the Appellate Court agreed with me that the Family Court mistakenly dismissed my petitions without conducting hearings and erred in granting Darius's motions to dismiss allegations made in my petitions. It also agreed that the Family Court wrongly sanctioned me by granting Darius sole legal custody of the children without even making an effort to determine whether there had been a change in circumstances.

"Given these concerns, Family Court's previous order must be reversed, and the matter remitted for a new hearing before a different judge," the Appellate Court wrote.

And there was more!

"Although a new hearing must be held on the father's violation petition, we nevertheless feel compelled to comment on the impermissible sanction that Family Court imposed upon the mother after finding that she willfully violated the order of custody and parenting time. Generally, the only available penalty that Family Court may impose for a willful violation of a custodial order without a concurrent modification petition pending is a monetary fine and/or a period of imprisonment. However, Family Court sanctioned the mother by modifying the joint legal order of custody and granting the father sole legal custody of the children without determining whether there had been a change in circumstances. In addition, Family Court failed to engage in any discernible analysis of whether a modification was in the best interests of the children."

"The orders further reveal that rather than accept the mother's allegations as true, Family Court improperly made factual findings and credibility determinations, inappropriately resolving the conflicting versions of events, as set forth in the mother's petitions and the father's supporting affidavits, against the mother and in favor of the father."

"The Appellate Court wiped away three of Sinclair's orders and sent the matters back for further proceedings before a different judge!" I said joyfully. "Finally! Victory!"

"Wow, Maria, you did good work! Good for you sticking with this," Jackie said. "Of course, I knew you would," she added with a huge grin.

"Now, I need Willowbrook County courts to do the right thing and execute the decision. At least Judge Reynolds corrected the record almost immediately when he received the Appellate Court's decision," I said. "What worries me is the flaw in the system. I mean, let's face it, they screwed up big time, and now they know it, but my case is going to go right back to the same court to be heard again. Is there anything to prevent them from making the same mistake twice? I don't understand why the appellate court can't simply finalize their decision and issue their own verdict."

"I have asked the same question," Jackie said. "This whole system needs an overhaul. Plus, these are supposedly smart people. Don't they see how what they're doing is creating the opportunity for future injustices?"

"They must. I learned there are no repercussions if the lower court fails to comply with their ruling. Can you believe that?" I asked.

"Honestly, I can," Jackie said, raising one eyebrow. "Why do you think I've been jerked around in the court system for fifteen years? A lot of people are getting paid every time these cases come back around. They're not inclined to fix the system even though they see how broken it is. Money talks."

After securing these three victories in my appeals, Laura Thompson told me she was losing every case before Judge Sinclair. Consequently, she suggested I withdraw my three appeal victories, promising to assist me in filing new petitions.

"Why would I do that? I had to pay for all that, and they have been resolved," I said.

"It's not a big deal, Maria. I will help you with new petitions," she said.

Confused, I said, "But that makes no sense.

I called my appeals attorney for her opinion about what Laura was advising me to do.

"I think your best course of action is to fire her," Moneek said.

In the meantime, I learned a new judge was assigned to the case from an adjoining county. He was proven to be an exemplary judge who showed genuine concern for the children involved. Deep down, I knew that withdrawing was not a wise decision. Why erase from the record not one but three monumental decisions from the appellate court? It simply didn't make sense.

Despite my immense respect and admiration for Laura, I opted to part ways with her. I felt terrible knowing she was suffering because of my victories, yet I was also unwilling to relinquish my hard-earned successes. I needed to be honest with her, and thankfully, she understood.

With Laura's blessing, I chose to represent myself.

Soon after, I filed a 440 motion to vacate the Willowbrook County Court's judgment, convicting me of possessing a forged instrument. I based the motion on the ineffective assistance of counsel I received in the case, specifically during plea discussions. My goal was to delete the criminal proceedings from my background completely. Here's how it all went down.

First, my criminal defense attorney never explained that the case would have been dismissed by accepting the ACOD. Instead, he repeatedly told me that he would win at trial, keep my criminal record clean, and maintain my reputation in the community.

Second, he also did not discuss with me the risk that if I went to trial and was convicted, I would face a sentence of up to seven years in jail. If I had fully understood the meaning of an ACOD, I would never have gone to trial. I can't imagine that any reasonable person would. The attorney never discussed the ACOD offer made by the district attorney and never explained why I should accept it. Proceeding to trial was a gross deviation from accepted professional standards. No counsel would advise their client to reject the plea agreement of an ACOD under the circumstances and proceed to trial.

In the end, despite their underestimations, Darius's relentless determination transformed our divorce into a twisted criminal case. It seemed to me that his singular objective was to tarnish my reputation by manipulating the very system that was meant to uphold justice. He sought to coerce the state of New York into funding his vendetta, sparing no expense to ensure my conviction. I believe that in his twisted logic, my refusal to reconcile after his betrayal became a justification for his malicious crusade. If he couldn't have me, then no other man would—his twisted rationale aimed to confine me, both physically and emotionally. But through it all, I emerged steadfast and resilient, refusing to be defined by his vindictive schemes.

"And that is exactly why I am going to move forward myself. I don't even have a law degree, and at this point, it appears I know more than they do."

"Bring it on," Laura said.

Chapter Twelve

ENDURANCE

"Success is not final, failure is not fatal: It is the courage to continue that counts."

Winston Churchill

As I prepared for what I hoped was the final battle, I armed myself with the determination I needed to finally reclaim my voice and my life.

The weeks I spent in the quiet solitude of the Willowbrook Law Library became the foundation for my resolve. After dismissing all but one attorney, I embarked on a journey of self-representation. It was time for me to step into my power and rewrite the narrative of my own life.

I approached the courtroom experience with a meticulously strategized approach, one that was honed over countless hours. At home in my living room, with poster-sized sheets meticulously divided into columns, I predicted and dissected Darius's arguments. Scouring my notes and drawing upon my experiences, I contemplated the most strategic way to question and respond.

Three trials unfolded simultaneously. The first lasted three grueling days, the second five even longer days, and the last and final battle only one. Each moment of each day, I embraced my unwavering resolve to shine a spotlight on the injustices doled out by what I had come to see as a broken system.

As I brought Darius to the stand and questioned him with clarity of purpose, I finally understood the wisdom in my cousin Jammy's words.

"To beat a crook, you must think like a crook."

It was at that moment that I understood my honesty and integrity were my greatest weapons.

With each objection raised, and each argument countered, I refused to succumb to the intimidation tactics of Darius's legal team. As the trial reached its climax, my case was grounded in fact and devoid of emotion, making it even more compelling. With the money I was making from my efforts of building a personal and corporate cleaning business, I spent hundreds of dollars on transcripts from all previous trials and used them as exhibits to prove my points. I exposed the ongoing discrimination and unfairness, displaying mistakes and injustices that favored Darius at the expense of my children's well-being.

With the purchased list of court appearances, I could recall almost verbatim what happened in each, making it easy to request the transcripts I would need. I was determined to use their own words against them and finally win my case.

Do your best to follow along as I reveal what happened in each court while keeping in mind that this was all happening at once. The level of stress in preparing a case that educated professionals hadn't been successful with was insane. On top of all that, I couldn't help but count the wasted hours that I could have spent running my business and being a mom.

As I read through the transcripts, I began to notice how often the judges were distracted by the minutia and compliments Darius piled on. As I focused on building my case, it appeared to me that his points became convoluted and confusing. Adding a large dollop of charm seemed to coax the judges to his side. It became clearer and clearer that if I were to win my cases, I would need to remain unemotional and stick to the facts. Using verbatim transcripts would prove my points.

In Family Court, there were two separate cases with two separate judges—one for custody and the other for child support. If you remember, I had just won three appellate decisions, and my attorney wanted me to withdraw. Once you win an appeal decision, the lower court has 45 days to commence the case.

> JUDGE: So, I was assigned to this matter. The Appellate Division issued their Decision, and in it, they said that the matter was going to be heard by another Family Court Judge. The language of the decision set proceedings to be commenced within 45 days of the date of this court's decision. That doesn't give us a lot of time for a hearing. I'd like to get this case resolved. Is that a possibility, counsels?

I had a good feeling about the judge—he was a dad who seemed to have compassion, plus, being from a different county, he was impartial. He also knew I was unafraid to go to the Appellate Court since I had just won three decisions from there.

An extenuating circumstance is that this was all happening during the pandemic, so the calls were made on the phone. On this call were the judge, my attorney (the only one I kept), myself, three law guardians, and Darius and his attorney.

> MY ATTORNEY: We may be able to resolve in Lieu of a proceeding. What I discussed was

having all parties withdraw all petitions that had been filed and that we go back to the original order that was in effect before Judge Sinclair granted the father sole custody. I briefly mentioned it to my client, but she didn't know that was something that was on the table.

No longer willing to be a doormat, I quickly jumped in. I would not go along with what they said to make it easier on them.

ME: Hang on for a second. I'm texting my attorney right now!

I grabbed my phone and started typing.

"I am not interested in withdrawing my victories in the Appellate Court. There are orthodontic issues and outstanding medical bills that need to be resolved," I wrote.

MY ATTORNEY: Judge. Why don't we do this? There are subsequent support matters that were decided based on the previous judge's decision. So, obviously, this court doesn't have jurisdiction over money issues. But if I'm trying to have a discussion with my client while everybody's on the call, it's a bit of an injustice to her.

Darius immediately jumped in.

DARIUS: I don't mean to jump into the conversation but there are no support matters outstanding.

I countered him.

ME: There most certainly are outstanding support matters. We have the braces issue that has been outstanding and drawn out for the past four years. That issue is in question.

DARIUS: The Magistrate had made the decision, and that case is over.

As you're reading, take note that this is where it all gets interesting.

ME: No. The judge put it on hold, waiting for the other judge's decision. Since the Appellate Court overruled that judge's decision, it was put on hold and is still on hold.

Now, it was my attorney's turn to jump in.

MY ATTORNEY: Yes, Judge. There are support issues now that the decision has been overturned. The father, per the parties' judgment or subsequent Support Order, has pro rata shares that he needs to pay for uncovered medical expenses. One of the issues was braces. My client is owed over $5,000.

JUDGE: So, over $5,000?

MY ATTORNEY: Yes. It would be over $5,000 because the Magistrate did not make the father pay his share. Based on the previous judge deeming a violation that the Appellate Court has now overturned, the money is owed to my client.

JUDGE: Ok, so let's pick a hearing date because I am under the gun!

Imagine five attorneys plus a Judge trying to coordinate their calendars while we're all on the phone.

JUDGE: I'm going to make somebody unhappy. I've got an Appellate Court Decision, and one of these judges is my former boss. So, he'll definitely give me a hard time. Let's see...

The judge picked a date and was met with several voices simultaneously.

JUDGE: I'm sorry. I hear two voices. Did someone have something to say? I didn't hear it. Elizabeth, did you say something?

On the one hand, the whole scene was quite entertaining, but on the other hand, it was very annoying.

So, this is how a court system rolls when its focus should be on the best interest of the children? What a joke, I thought.

The hearing was scheduled for a month later.

In the meantime, keep in mind what Darius said. "The Magistrate made the decision, and that case is over."

Four years earlier, when I paid for my daughter's braces and filed a violation for nonpayment of his pro rata, according to the transcripts that I purchased for close to nine hundred dollars, the Magistrate was clear.

MAGISTRATE: OK, so I am adjourning this violation because I can't rule on the braces orthodontic issue until there's a ruling by the other judge. It's without prejudice for you to file again on the violation concerning the braces because that matter is before the other judge. Do you understand Ms. Crowe? Your rights are preserved. But I'm not going to pre-judge the case prior to the other judge making a decision.

ME: I do understand, Your Honor, but it's more than just braces—it's support matters. Medical co-pays and owed support. This violation and petition were filed first long before Mr. Crowe filed the other petition. In your last order, dated three years ago, if you go to page 2 of your own order, we had the same issues with the orthodontist bill. It was part of your order. Also, back then, he owed support for the other children. My concern is that every time he doesn't want to pay, he comes up with excuses, playing courts against each other and stalling. Each time, I end up not getting the money owed when your order clearly states that he is responsible for eighty-three percent of any unreimbursed expenses. We end up back here every time. He doesn't want to pay because you refuse to violate him. So, it's as if your order means nothing.

MAGISTRATE: Well, my order is clear. Unreimbursed reasonable and necessary health care related expenses 83 percent and 17 percent. So, he might be saying something else in front of the other judge. I have no way of knowing. But I am going to wait. My order stands. He owes his percentage, you owe yours. I'm not going to try the issue right now. But my order definitely stands.

It was almost exactly the same dialogue as four years earlier. I am once again in front of the same Magistrate, asking him to rule on the same violation as four years earlier. And all this after an Appellate Decision had overturned everything. And still, nothing was resolved.

In addition to my violation petition, I filed a modification because we now had kids in college.

"They can work and pay for their own college," Darius had said when I broached the topic. "It's good for them to learn a solid work ethic and take care of their own bills."

In what I could only see as a retaliatory move, Darius requested a dismissal of my petition and filed a motion for temporary relief to reduce child support, claiming he had lost his job and that the braces matter had been resolved. He also filed a motion for constructive emancipation. (In New York, parents are obligated to pay basic child support and add-on expenses for their child until the child turns 21, unless the child is "emancipated" before he or she turns 21.)

JUDGE: She has the right to proceed on the petition. I'm going to ask you to file your own regular petition under the forms rather than doing it as a motion, a cross-petition motion. The sooner you file that, the better.

Once again, it appeared the judge was giving Darius legal advice.

JUDGE: You have to make sure you serve Ms. Crowe. I'm taking her entire document as an answer to her petition, and now that there are college issues as well, there are a lot of different things that come into play. This new petition deals with owing for braces. And to be quite honest, it's hard for me to review entire files. I have so many cases. But the braces have something about a transcript and an Appellate Court decision.

ME: Your honor, we were before you for this once, and you said because Mr. Crowe filed a violation against me for this same matter before another judge, you were going to wait until that judge ruled. And you stated that if I was in violation, then it would be pointless to have him pay and then give me the money back. So, you were going to wait and preserve my rights. We went through all that four years ago. And on that day, I said to you that I would be back with the transcripts to remind you of what you said because this keeps happening. You stated back then that your order stands by itself, and if he owes, you are going to make him pay. Well, here we are again. Having to go through another trial.

JUDGE: Alright, you are starting to freeze...

Darn this fucking pandemic! I hate being on Zoom for this! This is so frustrating, I thought.

JUDGE: I think I got the gist of what you are saying. The petition for braces that I dismissed because of the other judge ruling on it. Was that your petition, Mr. Crowe? Or hers?

ME: It was mine, Your Honor. It was my petition against him.

JUDGE: For what?

ME: For non-payment of unreimbursed medical expenses for the braces. But you put this on hold.

JUDGE: Well, we dismissed it.

ME: Yes.

JUDGE: So, you're now claiming what you claimed back then.

ME: Correct.

JUDGE: All right. I get it.

ME: That is it.

Darius jumped in once again, telling the judge that we had just been before the new judge assigned by the Appellate Court.

DARIUS: The braces issue was resolved.

ME: It's two different courts and two different matters. He is trying once again to mix oranges and apples to complicate and delay the matter even more.

JUDGE: I get it.

ME: Like he did before. Which is why we are still here.

JUDGE: I get it. I'm not trying to cut you short. I understand. I will review all the orders and documents to decide what is accurate and what's not. Mom's petition for enforcement on the braces issue at this point is still viable, and the petition to file a modification seeking an increase in support and college contribution is also still viable at this point. Mr. Crowe, you have the right to file a motion to seek dismissal based on the grounds you are claiming. We are going to give you a further proceedings date.

The date was issued.

In the meantime, in addition to these two court appearances and matters before two separate courts, I was also granted the hearing on the 440 Motion.

Things were finally going my way.

Simultaneously, I was working hard to build my business so I could afford to pay for my son's college. I was also working on launching *EmPowerHer with Maria,* so I was busy getting my coaching certification. After everything I had been through, my new passion was to help others overcome negative thinking and to teach people what I learned from my experiences. I also continued studying the word of God. It gave me such peace to know that even when my anxiety levels went through the roof, I could find solace in reading the stories of the Bible.

Behind the scenes, the attorney handling my custody issues continued to insist that I withdraw my three Appellate Court victories.

"We can buy the court more time," she said.

"I don't give a rat's ass if the court needs more time," I said. "They have had plenty of time to make things right over the last ten years. Instead, they wasted my money, ruined my reputation, and wrecked my career. I will not give up my three victories after all I have been put through."

Soon afterward, everyone was online on Skype.

JUDGE: We were scheduled to have a hearing today, but attorney Laura Thompson filed an order to show cause to be relieved. He is asking for a stay. I also received an affirmation from Maria in opposition to the request for the withdrawal. Did you all get copies of the documents?

All of the attorneys answered: "Yes."

JUDGE: I have to comment on a couple of things. The first is the objections filed by Maria. Just to make the record clear, I was called by the county's office around August 18th asking if I would accept this case because there was a reversal decided by the Appellate Court entered August 13th. I said yes, of course I would. After I said yes, I saw that I had 45 days to commence the proceedings because of all the delays. So, I take that language very seriously. I also want to put some context to this. In the world of COVID that we're in right now, the case I had just before this one was rushed along because of the mandate. Then, I got a letter from Mr. Crowe's attorney asking for an adjournment. I understand the pressure of the timing but that is not putting me or anyone under the gun. I'm the one who I feel is under pressure to go ahead with this matter. When I read the attorney memorandum as to why she was withdrawing, I felt like she was placed in a situation where she wasn't prepared to go forward. It seemed like a valid issue. That said, there's nothing I could do about it because I had 45 days to execute. So, with all that said, it sounds from reading Maria's papers that she's very pleased with the relationship between herself and her attorney. It did not sound from the attorney's papers that you were having a breakdown in communication. It was just that you were trying to explain what we had talked about in terms of timing and preparation time. The solution that came up was to avoid the 45 days when everyone would withdraw their petitions without prejudice, meaning they could refile them with new allegations. I have no problem if that's what everyone wants to do. I just want to make it clear if anybody wants to add anything.

ME: I'd like to, Your Honor.

JUDGE: Yes. Please go ahead.

ME: With all due respect, Your Honor, and to respect all attorneys that are present and that have been stated at the beginning of this conversation and as I stated in my papers, my attorney, in my opinion, is the best attorney in this county. I don't think that it is fair that because of all these abrupt changes in decisions with timing, that all of a sudden, I'm being put in a position where I have to lose my attorney. According to the last paragraph of the order from the Appellate Court, the case has to commence. It has already commenced. This is the part that I don't understand. Why, all of a sudden, am I being given two choices? Why do I need to waive my rights from the Appellate Court in order to do this 45 in days? The order doesn't say the case has to be finished within 45 days. It specifically says that it must commence within 45 days. It is not my fault or anyone else's fault, for that matter, that you were brought in from another county. I don't think it's fair to penalize me or to have to lose my attorney or put pressure on my attorney to have the case ready for a trial within a week when she was given the file basically two days before the 2nd hearing. I'm also confused because during the first hearing that we had over the phone, things were being thrown at me via e-mail. I communicated to the group that I wasn't able to check my email while on the call. Add to that you were trying to get me to come up with or agree to an agreement that I said I was not interested in doing. It was supposed to be scheduled for a hearing. In the nine years that we've been in this court, this has never happened before. Now that I've won, you're asking me to withdraw to give Your Honor and the attorneys more time. In the last paragraph, it reads that it must commence. It has commenced already. I am the petitioner here.

JUDGE: I just have to.

I cut him off.

ME: So...

JUDGE: Yes, Maria, I guess you could read that differently. My perception of what that last paragraph means is that the hearings are remitted, and said proceedings mean the hearings being commenced. I mean, obviously, this case is commenced. It was commenced years ago. I think what they mean, though, is that I need to have the hearing on these issues that were remitted within 45 days. That's how I read it.

ME: With all due respect, Your Honor, I spoke with the Appellate Court myself, and they said...hold on a moment. Let me read it because I took notes. They said, quote I don't understand why everyone is freaking out about this unquote.

JUDGE: I am not freaking out about it. Who did you talk to? I'd like to talk to that person.

ME: Yes, I spoke with... (Judge cut me off)

JUDGE: Because if it's accurate, yup, go ahead.

ME: I spoke with John Bacardi.

JUDGE: How do you spell that?

ME: I don't know how his last name is spelled. I didn't ask him. But phonetically, it's Bacardi. To me, it's sounded like the drink, Bacardi.

JUDGE: And who is he?

ME: He's the motions attorney in the Appellate Court.

JUDGE: OK. Well, if he is speaking for the Appellate Division, then they believe that the proceeding has already commenced. I'm not sure why that language, the hearing on the three petitions, says it must be commenced within 45 days. To me, that means the hearings have been delayed long enough. You must schedule the hearings. And I get that. It makes sense to me. But in your paragraph 17, you say it's my fault that I waited 37 days to schedule the first conference. That's not accurate. It was not my fault. It is also not your fault and that is why I was suggesting that everybody withdraw their petitions and refile them with new allegations because that would give us the time. Which means I don't have a 45-day mandate. That's the only reason I suggested it.

ME: Your Honor, with all due respect, I sent you...

The judge interrupted me again.

JUDGE: You don't have to say that.

ME: I do. You are a judge, and I respect that.

JUDGE: OK.

MY ATTORNEY: Maria, may I interrupt you for one second? I'm just going to say I think Maria has a misunderstanding. I tried to explain the time frame thing. The Appellate Division's decision would not go away regardless of whether she agreed to withdraw or not. We all know that Maria's petitions were dismissed prior to a hearing and never heard or tried before. We did have a good report during the trial. It was pre-COVID. It was a year and a half ago. I had a full staff at the time. Unfortunately, due to the shutdowns and reopening, you know I am somewhat limited now. Maria's petitions were never heard. It was only Mr. Crowe's petitions that were heard. We never provided witness lists with respect to her three cases. We never provided exhibit lists. I never received the file from the court until two days before the hearing and then that's when Your Honor said that we have one week from that day for trial. I'm trying to do what is best for my client. It really irked me to have to file this motion to withdraw, and I apologize that our time has been so limited.

ME: It pains me greatly as well, but I am not going to withdraw and waive my rights that the Appellate Court just gave me because everybody needs time. It would cost even more money than just giving another week or two so that the attorneys can properly prepare for the trial.

JUDGE: Yes, I have no problem with that. None. As I continue reading the mandate, I think what they are saying is that everybody would be prepared. So, the time to prepare would start then. If everyone puts on the record that they consent not to be bound by the 45 days, I believe Maria, you're absolutely right. That would be in your best interest, and it would probably avoid an appellate issue down the line. It's not that I'm trying to pressure you or that I forgot the language you used, but I took a little offense to it. It's not that I'm an emotional person. It's just I was given a directive from the Appellate Division that I'm going to follow. But if you guys want to put that on the record, I will agree to extend it.

ME: Your Honor, it was not against you. When I wrote "Court," it wasn't directed at you in particular. It was Family Court in general.

JUDGE: Well, I think the quote is Family Court needs to buy time. Let's pick a date that works for everyone for a hearing.

DARIUS: I'm sorry, this is Mr. Crowe. I hate to interrupt, but my attorney just lost connection.

JUDGE: Oh shoot, I just noticed that.

The attorney calls back and connects.
"I've been gone for the past two minutes," he said.

JUDGE: Ok, so let me address a couple of issues. Maria, I got your objections. You don't want your attorney to be relieved, right? You still want her to be your attorney, correct?

ME: That is correct, Your Honor.

JUDGE: Attorney Thompson, if given enough time, you have no problem continuing as Maria's attorney, correct?

My ATTORNEY: That is correct.

JUDGE: All right then. Does everyone have any objections if we go beyond the 45 days?

Everyone agreed, and a court date was set for December 18th.
Darius interrupted again.

DARIUS: Well, I would just like to chime in. This is Mr. Crowe. You know Ms. Crowe is right. It's been nine years of being in court. I think I speak for everyone in saying I really don't think we need nine more. So, it would be nice if this could be resolved so we can continue with smooth sailing.

Always the charmer. I would love to beat the shit out of you! We've only been in court this long because you've been refusing to pay! I thought, feeling my face redden. Taking a deep breath, I continued.

ME: I just want everyone to keep in mind that we're here because of the best interest of the children. I know that the kids want mom and dad, and that's why we split time 50/50. They're at an age where they do have a voice, and I would like their voices to be heard. It's not about Maria. It's not about Darius. It's about the three kids that have been paying the price for the past nine years.

JUDGE: Sadly, I think a lot of time, the kids don't necessarily recognize how much time is spent with each parent or all those other issues. They just want to see their parents interact nicely, to be able to say, 'Hey, Mom did great things for us, and dad reacts with wow, that's awesome; you know you're very lucky to have your mom.' That kind of language goes a long way. So, let's pick a date.

==/==

At that point, as much as I loved and respected my attorney, I decided to represent myself moving forward. No one knew my story better than I did, and with my new resolve to find my own voice, it seemed like the right thing to do.

It was January when we appeared in court again.

We put the case on the record and scheduled another date for a trial. It was more of the same— pushing the case months out.

I stood up to represent myself.

COURT: Ms. Crowe, do you wish to have an attorney represent you in this matter?

ME: I do not, Your Honor.

COURT: If that changes, would you let me know?

ME: Yes, I will.

COURT: Okay. And there are three attorneys, one for each child. Let's schedule a hearing. Don't expect anything groundbreaking to come from my decision. Thankfully, these are minor Family Court things.

ME: Well, Your Honor....

COURT: Yes.

ME: I'm confused about your statement. You are saying they are minor.

COURT: They are. Spend a week in Family Court, and you will see what I mean. We deal with people who are abusing their children. Your issues are minor.

ME: No! I don't think anyone has read my petition. Most of it is about my 14-year-old attempting to commit suicide three times.

COURT: I did not read that in your petition.

ME: That is what my petition is about! My child needs help, and her father is sabotaging her getting treatment, interfering in the mental health process, and threatening to sue the therapists. This is not minor. This is serious.

COURT: What petition are you referring to? I don't have that petition.

ME: The only petition that I filed. It was signed and stamped by Your Honor on December 8th at 11:04 AM. There are also exhibits attached to it.

DARIUS'S ATTORNEY: And that, Maria, I think, oops, I'm sorry, I don't have permission to call you by your first name. I do have the petition you are referring to.

COURT: I apologize to you, Ms. Crowe. I do not have a copy of that petition. Even though, apparently, I stamped it. So, I will get a copy of it. Are these recent attempts?

ME: Yes, Your Honor.

COURT: Ms. Sydney, are you aware of this?

LAW GUARDIAN: I am, Your Honor, and I have spoken to my client.

DARIUS'S ATTORNEY: I don't want to make light of the allegations involving a young woman's health, but when we talk about suicide attempts, these were not actual attempts. There was no harm inflicted.

ME: Actually, you are incorrect. I'm going to stop you right now because you didn't see my daughters' wrists cut up. You didn't talk to the therapist. You have no idea what you are saying. And this, Your Honor, is why we need to go to trial. Her father does this every single time, and everyone believes him and his side only, regardless of the facts and evidence. He himself needs a psychological evaluation. Instead of co-parenting like any normal parent who is concerned about their child, he fights and neglects the children's needs. He wants what he wants when he wants it. He is like Hitler. And this is why we can't get anything resolved. Co-parenting to him is him calling all the shots. Anything that I say is disregarded as if I'm an idiot. I haven't had a voice, and I'm tired of not being heard. I am not treated like a parent in this court. I basically am treated as someone who just birthed the babies, and the father gets all the control. But as we can see based on the facts in my petition, he has failed and failed miserably. And I cannot stand here and watch my kids suffer, watch their futures being ruined, and do nothing while they try to kill themselves. It's a cry for attention from the court that continues to be ignored. Nobody in this court system has ever listened to these kids.

COURT: Well, I have a hearing scheduled.

ME: It's frustrating.

COURT: I will meet the children, and I promise I will listen to them.

ME: Can you please be clear about what you will be listening to on the next appearance and what we are doing?

COURT: Are you seeking any immediate relief at this time?

LAW GUARDIAN: On a temporary basis, I would like the child to continue with the counselor that was selected by mom until we are here next time.

COURT: I just want to say, I find in my experience that the orders that are really specific like this one sometimes create more problems due to not allowing parents to be parents and adapt to changes as they come up. For example, let's say you would like to make a plan to go to Cordova for three weeks, and your child would like to go. But the order says two weeks. You two are mom and dad, the only two people on this planet who are mom and dad to these children. So, do whatever you think is right. If you have to file a violation because you can't cooperate, so be it. We'll be here.

The judge was making such a valuable point. I wanted more freedom and a willingness to discuss changes. But Darius had been completely inflexible up until then.

COURT: I look very young, but I am an old man. And I know you're going to realize that as you get older, the minutes on the clock don't matter. You could spend one day out of thirty and that's the day your daughter will remember because you had such a great time, you know? It's up to you. I mean, if you feel like it's got to be 50/50 to the second, so be it. But that's not my mindset.

DARIUS: I'm all for flexibility.

Again, I wanted to throw up.

Darius is all for flexibility? Since when? He's been nothing but inflexible since this whole thing started, which is why we are still in court after all these years.

The matter was adjourned for two more months.

In the meantime, the trial before the Magistrate for child support began. Keep in mind that Darius was filing a petition for a reduction of child support in addition to the emancipation of our son, which would relieve him from paying support for him. It was Darius's claim that he had lost his job and now was making less than before.

I was representing myself, and this time, Darius decided to represent himself as well. When the hearing commenced, it was just the two of us and the Magistrate still on Zoom since this all occurred during the pandemic. Even though my petitions were filed four years earlier and never heard, the judge allowed Darius to go first.

After we were both sworn in, the judge asked me to present my exhibits and any receipts pertaining to my claim. Then, he moved to Darius and his testimony.

Things got interesting quickly. Imagine two people who have been in court nearly every week for nine years finally having the opportunity to question each other.

ME: Your Honor, I would like to ask if Mr. Crowe could refrain from making his sarcastic faces. I can see his face up close right on my phone, and it's very distracting. Every time I make a comment or have a question, he makes sarcastic faces. It's really not professional or appropriate."

JUDGE: Alright. Please try to stay civil as much as possible. I would appreciate that.

During Darius's testimony, he painted a picture of a man making a substantial amount of money suddenly lowered to a position that was paying significantly less.

DARIUS: Our son is refusing to stay at my house. He insists he wants to live with his mother. I believe it's because, like my stepson, when our son graduated from high school, I suggested he take a gap year from college since he doesn't enjoy being a student.

ME: I object to that, Your Honor.

JUDGE: It's irrelevant what the stepson did.

I practiced the word "objection" over and over until it was carved into my brain and became an automatic response. Raising an objection provides the opportunity to explain. Then, the judge immediately agrees or overrules.

Any time Darius dragged up a point I knew was minutia or that I felt was his attempt to add insignificant information to complicate the matter, I objected.

ME: Your Honor, can you hear me?

JUDGE: Yes.

ME: Could I voir dire and ask him a question?

JUDGE: Yes.

(I had no idea what "voir dire" meant, but Darius kept using it, and I wanted to see if the judge would grant me the same right.)

JUDGE: Ms. Crowe, you'll definitely be able to ask him questions about this when it is your turn to cross-examine. The voir dire is whether I think it's relevant material to come in as an exhibit. But write your notes and questions down. When he finishes, you can ask him about anything related to this exhibit.

ME: During my testimony, Mr. Crowe voir dire everything that I said regardless of whether it was an exhibit or not.

JUDGE: I don't know what you are talking about, but.

ME: Okay.

JUDGE: The purpose of voir dire is before I enter it as an exhibit. But if it's a certified business record, it automatically gets entered. If he tries to use a text message or something along those lines, before I would admit it, I would ask, 'Do you want to voir dire, which means, do you want to ask questions about it? That's my purpose, OK?

ME: Okay.

JUDGE: You had the right terminology, but in this case, it's a certified business record. But you certainly don't waive any right to ask him questions about it, as you were starting to do. You only need to wait until he finishes his testimony.

(I was determined to point out any inclination of favoritism that was taking place during this trial. Because I knew that the stenographer was creating a transcript to prove what took place, I was careful to point out anything Darius was allowed that I was not.)

That night after court, I told my friend, Jackie, "I studied the term and definition. In a Family Court proceeding, *voir dire* typically refers to a process where one party questions a witness to determine their qualifications, credibility, or the admissibility of their testimony after they have testified. If there is a question about whether certain evidence or testimony should be admitted, voir dire can be used to clarify the foundation of that evidence."

"That's interesting," Jackie said. "I've never heard of it before."

"I don't think many people have unless they have spent time in the court system. I was using the term not knowing what it meant because Darius kept using it," I said, giggling. "What I learned is that if a party wants to be sure a document is authentic or relevant before it's accepted into evidence, they use voir dire as a tool to challenge or validate."

The following day, an instance came up where the judge would not allow my daughter's college receipt since no court order stipulated splitting college expenses. But when Darius was testifying and had only one receipt, the judge allowed it. I jumped on the opportunity to point out favoritism.

> ME: "I wasn't allowed to talk about my daughter's college expenses or present any receipts connected to the expense. Why is he allowed to present this one?

> JUDGE: "Yes, you're right, Ms. Crowe. Mr. Crowe, please refrain from introducing any exhibits related to your daughter's college."

"If I had not questioned that and put the judge on the spot, he would have allowed him to continue testifying. And he would have accepted the exhibit!" I said to Jackie that evening.

"Good for you, Maria. You're doing an amazing job of standing up for yourself," Jackie said.

Honestly, the situation became comical at points because I kept objecting to comments as he tried to fabricate realities that were not so. In one instance, Darius presented a picture of our son to the judge.

> ME: I object to that, Your Honor.

> JUDGE: What's your basis of objection? You can voir dire if you want to ask him questions about it. You have the right to do that.

> ME: My objection, Your Honor, is that the picture could be staged.

DARIUS: I'm testifying that it is not.

JUDGE: Who took the photo?

DARIUS: I did.

In another instance, while Darius was testifying, he was creating a dialogue that I found objectionable.

DARIUS: He told me that they had.

ME: Objection. My son is not here to say whether he said that or not.

JUDGE: Correct, that would be hearsay.

After many hours I finally had the opportunity to question him about the money for our daughter's braces.

DARIUS: Your Honor, I'm going to object again to these things that are, I don't know, how many years old. I don't see the relevance.

ME: Your Honor, this petition is four years old. It's four years old because he delayed it, and so did this court. But this information is relevant, and he needs to answer yes or no. That was my question.

JUDGE: Just say yes or no. If it's a no, just say no. You don't need to object. She can ask these questions. If the answer is yes, say yes or answer the question the best you can. Do you understand the question, Mr. Crowe?

ME: Did you file a violation against Ms. Crowe after she took your daughter to a psychologist recently?

DARIUS: I object and refuse to answer that. It's irrelevant.

JUDGE: What's the relevance here?

ME: Your Honor, he keeps stalling by throwing violations in court when he doesn't want to pay. We're here four years later. He went to other courts and did the exact same thing. He stalls so he doesn't have to pay.

JUDGE: We're here now. At your closing, you can make that comment if you want, but now he doesn't have to answer.

The trial went on for hours. Finally, we got to the closing.

ME: My recent petition was filed over four years ago. They were dismissed several times but the most recent one was kept. When I first came to this court for the braces violation, the judge postponed my hearing for over a year and a half, and this court did absolutely nothing. It's been over four years now. The Appellate Court order speaks for itself. The judge was removed. I was not found in violation of the allegations that the father was claiming in his petition. That court did not agree with him, and later on, he withdrew that petition. That petition had nothing to do with child support. That petition was before another judge and it had to do with custody. The braces payments were never before another judge. It was before this court four years ago, and today, I say the same thing that I said then. These transcripts speak for themselves. Why does he feel he should not have to pay his obligation as a father? He put the burden and the full debt on me. All my petitions have been ignored before this court. Then, to avoid paying for his son, who left his home because he couldn't stand to live with him anymore, the father files an emancipation petition claiming that his son abandoned him. He pretends and makes everyone believe that his household is a perfect household. It is very far from that. He disregards what any of the doctors say or what any of the court's protocols or demands are. An example of that is exactly what he did in his subpoena: he provided a subpoena, an answer to the court, and a blank statement. He did not comply with the subpoena. It's an unsigned letter that could have been written by anyone. He makes a mockery of this court. He is in this court to ruin my career and my chances for employment, and he claims that he's always worked. I've also always worked. But he tried to discredit me. He put me in jail to avoid paying child support. He ruined my career and my reputation. But here I am. I picked myself up and started over. I will clean a thousand toilets if need be to ensure that my kids will never go hungry. I would never abandon my children. The Appellate Court has made it very clear that my petitions were never heard. I filed and sought help from the court to help my kids, but I was ignored and discriminated against in this court. But I'm glad the Appellate Court saw the mistakes and blatant favoritism that were made by the judge and removed him. All my kids ever wanted was to be loved by their father. His testimony was downright disturbing. He attempted to discredit his own son and even attempted to portray him as committing a felony so he could avoid paying his parental responsibilities. It is no secret to anyone that my son struggled all these years. My son needed his medication, but when the father was granted legal custody by that other judge, he didn't want to pay for the co-pays, so he took him off his ADHD medication. Mr. Crowe didn't put my son's needs first. He just didn't want to pay for it.

JUDGE: Ms. Crowe, I have one question. Are you still interested in pursuing the motions for contempt?

ME: If he does not provide his paystubs, absolutely yes!

JUDGE: Mr. Crowe, you will provide your paystub to the court within the next two-week period.

Darius finally complied.

We were back in February for trial, seven months since the appellate court decision, after many appearances and zero resolution.

In the end, victory was finally mine. The judge saw through Darius's legal team's facade, recognizing the truth that had been hidden for far too long. With the dismissal of Darius's claims and the granting of child support owed, justice prevailed, and the interests of my children were finally prioritized.

Darius's attorney, Amanda Brooks, was forced to step down from the case due to impropriety standards.

"Every single time we were in court, Darius put her on social media both promoting each other. I saw it as an 'I'll scratch your back if you scratch mine' scenario," Maria said.

I filed a Motion to have her removed, and I won for impropriety standards. The judge granted my motion. We're on a 30-day stay of proceedings to allow Darius time to find a new lawyer."

"How do you feel about that, Maria?" Jackie asked.

"Well, the battle is now directly between Maria and Darius. Honestly, it feels good," Maria answered.

But the battle did not end there. As I navigated further legal challenges, including a motion 440 hearing before Judge Reynolds, I encountered setbacks, but I also experienced moments of unexpected compassion that gave me hope and helped keep my chin up during the rougher times.

The ADA that had agreed to overturn the criminal charges was promoted two days before the hearing and moved to another county. To my dismay, the original ADA, who had told my attorney, "I don't like Maria. I am not letting her go," returned to the case.

God made the impossible possible! I won my Motion 440--everything was overturned, and my record is now clean. Justice was finally served, all thanks to God's power. The Holy Spirit ignited within me a burning determination to reclaim my rightful place in the world.

During this time, I was faced with another profound loss: the sudden passing of my father, a man I loved deeply. When he was diagnosed with pancreatic cancer, I rushed to Cordova to be with him.

"What do you think, Daddy?" I asked after reading him the chapters on my jail stay and my courtroom experiences.

His eyes were soft when he said, "I am so happy your story is getting out there, Maria, my beautiful daughter. You are a woman of integrity, and you are honest and hardworking. God and Our Lady of Fatima are watching over you. They are as proud of you as I am." Then he put his hands together in a prayer position and said, "Amen."

The pain of the grief at his passing nearly took my breath away. As I worked through the heartache, I took solace in my memories of him. His belief in me served as a light in my darkest moments. I made it back to the United States a week and a half before the COVID world lockdown.

With my father's words as my anchor, I pressed forward, determined to honor his legacy and fulfill the dreams he held for me.

Although the light at the end of this tunnel seemed to be a long way off, thanks to my hard work and determination, I purchased a home for my children, which, to me, stood as a symbol of stability. Despite the jealousy and attempts of Darius to use it against me in court, I stood firm in my resolve to provide a stable environment for my three children, unwavering in my commitment to their well-being.

I often found myself grappling with a profound weariness—an exhaustion born not of physical exertion but of the relentless burden imposed by false accusations and malicious intent. I am weary of the ceaseless battle to erase the indelible stain that Darius's actions have left upon my name—a stain that threatens to overshadow my countless achievements and contributions to my community and beyond. It pains me to realize that my own children may be unaware of the depths of my accomplishments, their perception distorted by the shadow of trauma cast by their own father's malice.

Chapter Thirteen

TRANSFORMATION

"The only way to make sense out of change is to plunge into it, move with it, and join the dance."

Alan Watts

I came out of jail the second time, a different person. The system didn't "correct" or change me. Instead, the people and things I experienced opened my eyes to new perspectives and my heart to change.

Spending time locked up in jail offered me street smarts. It educated me about the politics of the legal system and taught me to be grateful for what I had. In my pre-jail life, I pretty much operated on autopilot. The experience taught me the value of living in the moment.

I credit this transformation process in large part to understanding the power of prayer. During my incarceration, I read every book of the Bible, but I especially loved Proverbs and the Book of Job, each of which I read at least fifty times. As I mentioned, I also read various inspiring authors on the topics of forgiveness and growth. Not a minute of my time went to waste.

Reading had a long-term effect on my psyche. I no longer just believed that God had my back—I felt it.

Do not be anxious about anything, but in every situation, by prayer and petition, with thanksgiving, present your requests to God. And the peace of God, which transcends all understanding, will guard your hearts and minds in Christ Jesus. Philippines 4:6-7

This verse taught me the difference between saying, 'I have faith,' and viscerally feeling the words with my heart and mind.

At my core, I held the same beliefs. I still stood firm in my roots as the daughter of hard-working immigrant parents who earned twenty-five cents an hour. They set high standards for me and built a strong foundation that helped me to succeed. That part of me remained intact. I continue to prefer to keep busy, spending quality time doing fun, family-oriented things.

Yet, I continually silently repeated a friend's advice, "You need to change your story." I repeated the phrase over and over until the true meaning finally sank in.

During that stressful period, I continually chanted, "I feel so stuck...I'll never get another job or have a normal life again..." like it was my mantra. I worried that my kids would suffer, and I clung to a negative outlook, continually using the word "never."

I'll never work in TV again. I'll never have my own house again. I'll never get my reputation back. I'll never be what I was before this all happened.

Thanks to my friend, I began to open up to new possibilities. It slowly became clear that my thoughts and words were creating my experience. That was when I suddenly realized that each one of us was creating our own reality every single day.

Creating a new story starts by breaking old thoughts and behavior patterns and forming new, more hope-filled thoughts. Because thoughts create such powerful energy, the outcome is enormous. As Proverbs 18:21 says, "Death and life are in the power of the tongue, and those who love it will eat its fruits."

On a cold December morning, I decided to get baptized for a second time. My friends and family couldn't understand.

"Maria, you were baptized as a baby. Why do you feel the need to be baptized again?" I was asked over and over again.

It would have been difficult to explain the call I was feeling. For me, baptism was about showing my gratitude and offering my thanks. Without the support I received through my faith, I honestly don't know if I would have gotten through everything that happened. Plus, I didn't care what anyone else thought. This was between me, God, and Jesus.

"It's just something I need to do," I answered.

The baptism took place at Summit Heights Church, a nondenominational organization in Meadow Park. During the ceremony, I was asked a question I had been thinking about nonstop.

"Do you accept Christ Jesus as your savior?"

"I do," I answered, feeling my body go warm and my eyes fill with tears of thanks.

As my physical body was submerged under the water, my soul felt more alive than it had ever felt before. The tears of joy that started that day continued for the next two weeks. I was overwhelmed with happiness and completely unafraid to express my faith to anyone who would listen. I was so grateful that despite having endured all those terrible experiences and injustices, I remained steadfast in my promise and faith.

Soon after my baptism, I hired the best appellate attorney I could find to write my appeal. Then, at 6 PM that same evening, my real estate agent called me with great news.

"Maria! Your offer was accepted!" she said. "The house is yours!"

"Yay! I'm a homeowner again!" I practically squealed as I danced around my kitchen. The house was everything I had pictured in my mind. I had seen the sunrise from my bedroom window and the sunset from my front door clearly in my mind before I found the house. The myriad of windows throughout offered wonderful light even on a rainy day. It was perfect.

That year was one of the best since the day I filed for divorce. By refusing to play the victim, I learned to reflect on every situation and take away the lessons presented.

While writing this book, I reflected on everything that had happened over the previous seven years. The weight of it hit me hard, maybe for the first time. That might sound crazy to you, but while I was in the middle of it, I had handed the heaviest part of the load to God. Throughout the entire experience, I prayed hard and a lot; I thanked God for everything I had, despite knowing everything I had lost. There was a pivotal moment during the worst of it when I was struck by a realization.

I have no control over any of this. But God has my back, and He will help me achieve what's best for me in this situation.

Although my core didn't change, I will admit that my personality did. First, I am more humble than I used to be. I have more patience with people, and I do my best to look at both sides of any argument. I have learned not to react in the moment but rather to listen to understand. I think my key takeaway is that self-awareness is critical. It's the key to everything.

Creating a persistently positive attitude began to occupy more and more of my thoughts. By focusing on the positive in every situation, my life circumstances began to turn around. Today, I have more than I ever had before, and even though I lost business during the pandemic, I never panicked. I knew for a fact that the business would come back to me. And it has.

Practicing positivity can carry you through just about any situation. One of the most important things that became clear through my ordeal is that as things evolve over time, your perspective changes. For instance, even though I was heartbroken when I lost my home after the divorce, one of the best things that ever happened to me was moving out of the house that Darius and I shared.

I don't have any regrets in my life. After thirteen years in the court system, I realized material things don't matter. Let's face it: you will never see a U-Haul behind a hearse!

I have lost everything and gained it back in spades because I have no attachment to money and the idea of a lack. There is always enough when you believe there is enough.

People complain about jobs, shoes, food, and clothes. I am here to tell you this: Stop complaining and appreciate the beautiful things that God has given us all—birds in the sky, beautiful clouds, life-giving trees, and the air that we breathe. Appreciate your kids. Appreciate your parents. Don't be afraid to tell them every day how much you love them. Focus your attention on your real friends, those who will be there for you no matter the situation, stand up for you, and defend and advocate for you if you've been wronged.

During the darkest days of my jail time, amidst the confines and uncertainties, I uncovered a profound truth: the value of life's smallest wonders, meticulously crafted by a higher power. From the humble ant scurrying to its nest to the majestic sunrise, sunset, and soft yet vibrant hues of a rainbow, I found solace and meaning in the simplicity of existence.

Before all this, I recoiled at the sight of ants, their tiny bodies causing me to jump and run. Yet, while in jail, a transformation occurred. Stepping into the confined outdoor space, I was met with towering barriers enclosing an expansive but limited space. The cracked cement under my feet became a sanctuary, a canvas for newfound appreciation.

It was there, in that isolated patch of ground, that I learned to put away my preconceptions. Seeing an ant there no longer caused me fear. Instead, I saw a fellow creature of this earth. For the first time in my life, I saw the ant as sacred—just as we all are.

With each passing day, I more closely embraced the simplicity of existence, relishing every moment spent beneath the open sky. I became a connoisseur of sunlight, soaking in its warmth with gratitude. During those short moments of confined freedom, I dug into the pages of borrowed books, plunging myself into tales of adventure and possibility.

In the darkest of moments, amidst the harshness of confinement, I discovered a profound truth: the light of appreciation can illuminate our souls even in the worst of times. And so, I left those walls not merely as an ex-convict but as a pilgrim of gratitude, forever indebted to the beauty of life's smallest treasures.

Live every minute in joy. Live each day as if it is your last.

In the narrative of my life, God is not just a presence; He is intricately woven into every detail of every moment.

All I ever desired was pure peace and a normal family. Sadly, I had the opposite. But I am so blessed with three beautiful, amazing kids. My sole aim has always been to provide for them and foster a strong family bond—to show them the essence of what it means to be family. Regrets over what could have or should have been serve no purpose now or ever. As this chapter closes, I hope to one day find my soulmate, someone who will connect with my heart and not just my outer shell. I hope for someone who makes me smile and someone with who I can share my secrets without fear of betrayal—a true best friend.

"I am with you always, to the very end."

- Matthew 28:20

Tips for Navigating the "Justice" System

Since launching "Family Matters" in 2009, Maria has advocated for children, families, and women. But now, after interviewing so many parents who have gone through or are now going through the same experiences Maria suffered, I see the need for real advocates who have suffered at the hands of the law and "justice" system.

During the writing of this story, Maria included in her notes tips that she felt would be helpful to anyone who find themselves stuck in the same situation. I suggested that we create a section in the book where she could outline them for the reader. She happily agreed!

1) In New York State, Family Court judges generally decide petitions involving children, such as child support and custodial rights. Supreme Court justices hear and decide motions dealing with finances.

2) It is important to know the courts and their different roles and functions. There are significant costs involved with making motions and seeking subpoenas in the Supreme Court, while it's generally free to file petitions in Family Court.

3) Selecting an attorney is probably the most important decision a person can make in a divorce or any legal matter. This can present a

whole list of challenges for a layperson going through a highly tumultuous time.

Before hiring an attorney, research their history. Read reviews posted online and find out the number of times they have gone to trial. Not every attorney knows family law or how to conduct themselves in a courtroom.

Be careful not to hire an attorney who tries to settle your divorce because they are not comfortable going to trial. Before signing any contract, ask yourself, "Do I believe this is a hardworking, capable attorney?"

It is also extremely helpful to know the background of the opposing lawyer in your case. You can go online to search news articles and client reviews. It is also extremely important to research any political campaign contributions they have made. This will help you get an idea of their political party affiliation, political connections, and who they have supported.

Political donations made and received are public information. Go to the New York State Board of Elections website to find out when the judge handling your case was elected and who financially supported their campaign.

There is a lot of information online about judges, too. It is important to know what they stand for, their reputation, and their standing in the community.

You can also access information about an attorney or judge by conducting a cursory search on social media. There are Facebook groups dedicated to courtroom experiences.

4) Your attorney should explain in great detail why he/she suggests accepting a deal.
5) If you, a family member or a friend face legal problems in court, I strongly suggest you take time to sit in a relevant courtroom to observe

proceedings. This will give you a bird's eye view of how the system operates, giving you a better idea of what to expect.

Familiarize yourself with the fundamentals of any trial such as:

    a. Objection
    b. Exhibit
    c. Strike

Winning in the courtroom requires presenting facts and evidence, not emotions. Make sure you save all your receipts, checks, and transactions, and try to maintain a diary that tracks developments and things like the names of those you speak or meet with. A good attorney will use the saved items and enter them into the court as exhibits and evidence.

Judges do NOT care about how you feel.

Pay close attention to court dates and deadlines. Knowing your rights is vital, but in order to exercise those rights, you must meet crucial deadlines. Not doing so can cause you to face permanent consequences. For instance, you have thirty (30) days after a court decision to file an appeal. You forfeit the right to challenge a judge's ruling if that deadline expires.

Divorce cases are not intended to drag on for years. Know your rights.

6) Your demeanor will be judged in the courtroom, so find an activity that puts you in a calm state of mind. Unfortunately, when you are upset, it is possible that you may say something you don't mean or something that isn't helpful to your case. There are tools readily available for your use. A few examples are:

a. EFT (Emotional Freedom Technique), also known as Tapping, is a wonderful way to release stress and lessen anxiety. We will be holding workshops on EFT, but in the meantime, you will find lots of information about the technique online.

b. Meditation is another powerful tool for finding peace and staying calm in difficult situations. There are many meditation apps. They are also readily available on YouTube.

c. Positive Affirmations help keep your mind focused and in the moment. If you suddenly feel nervous or upset, have a chosen affirmation ready. An example may be, "I am calm and peaceful. I trust something bigger than me to handle all the details in an unseen and unknown way."

7) Learning to think clearly under duress takes time and practice. Keep in mind that staying in a negativity energy creates anxiety while staying in a positive energy helps keep you calm.

8) I compare the experience of being in jail to being on the television series, "The Survivor." Below are some survival (and beauty tips) for jail:

a. It's always loud in jail, so earplugs are helpful. You can craft a pair by removing cotton from the inside of a maxi pad and wrapping that with the outer layer of plastic from the pad.

b. To thread your eyebrows, use the string from tampons.

c. Pro Tip: You can use the string from tampons to floss your teeth.

d. Sleeping in jail can be difficult since some lights remain on so corrections officers can see while making security and health checks on prisoners. Put a maxi pad inside a bra and place it over your eyes to block the light.

e. The interior of jail cells can be ugly and depressing. Create colorful pictures and affix them to the wall with toothpaste.

f. If cold air is blowing from a vent in your cell, stab a pen through cardboard from the back of a writing pad and shove it in the vent. Just be sure to remove the device each morning before count so the corrections officers will not see it.

g. In jail, you are allowed two peanut butter and jelly sandwiches for lunch. Eat one for lunch and save the other for a snack!

h. Create a decent pillow by stuffing extra clothes inside your pillowcase. This can save you from a painful backache that can occur from sleeping on a flat pillow.

9) Your parole officer is not your friend. While they are with you, stay cool and do not offer any information unless you are specifically asked. An example is below.

Parole Officer: How is everything going?
You: Great.
Parole Officer: Has anything changed?
You: No.

Tips for Dealing with a Narcissist

Characteristics of a Narcissist in Divorce

1. Lack of Empathy: Narcissists often fail to understand or care about the emotional needs of others, even their own children. In Maria's case, her ex-husband's abandonment of his responsibilities toward their kids illustrates this clearly.
2. Blame Shifting: Narcissists rarely take responsibility for their actions. Instead, they shift the blame to others. Darius's letter accusing Maria of needing counseling to be "more cooperative and honest" is a classic example of this behavior. Not once did he take responsibility for his infidelity and abandonment.
3. Manipulation and Control: Narcissists often use manipulation to control the narrative. They may use gaslighting (making your question your reality) or play the victim. By putting Maria in jail to avoid paying child support, Darius demonstrated a willingness to manipulate the system for his benefit.
4. Lack of Accountability: Narcissists will go to great lengths to avoid consequences for their actions.

Darius's continued avoidance of child support, combined with the use of legal loopholes, is a beautiful example of this principle.

5. Grandiosity and Superiority: Narcissists have an inflated sense of self-importance and believe they are superior to others. An example of this is Darius's habit of framing himself as an upstanding citizen while trying to depict Maria as dishonest (for doing the same thing he did), reflects this concept perfectly.

6. Entitlement: Narcissists often believe they are entitled to special treatment, whether it is financial, emotional, or legal. Darius demonstrated his entitlement to avoid his child support obligations regardless of the harm it caused.

7. Deception: Lying or distorting the truth is common, especially when it comes to maintaining a certain image or avoiding repercussions. Infidelity, abandonment, and using legal strategies to harm Maria both financially and emotionally are clear examples.

8. Triangulation: Narcissists may involve third parties, such as attorneys or mutual friends, to bolster their position and create division. By using the same attorney who was removed from the case previously, Darius may have been attempting to triangulate the situation and create further stress.

9. Emotional and Psychological Abuse: Beyond the legal and financial manipulation, narcissists often engage in emotional abuse, leaving their victims feeling confused, worthless, and drained. The stress of enduring court battles and false accusations can lead to severe emotional trauma.

Navigating Divorce with a Narcissist

Navigating divorce with a narcissist can be exhausting and cause mental, physical, and emotional distress. Below are a few points that can help you deal with the situation in a less stressful manner.

Set Boundaries: It is crucial to establish and maintain firm boundaries, as narcissists will often attempt to violate them.

Don't Engage in Their Games: Narcissists thrive on conflict and emotional reactions. Responding with calm, factual statements rather than engaging in emotional arguments can prevent them from gaining control.

Document Everything: Keep detailed records of all interactions, legal proceedings, and financial matters, as narcissists often distort the truth.

Seek Legal Support: Find legal professionals experienced in dealing with narcissistic behavior in divorce cases, as they can anticipate manipulative tactics.

Self-Care and Support: Dealing with a narcissist is emotionally draining, so prioritize your mental health. Surround yourself with supportive people, seek therapy and practice self-care.

Maria and I hope that you will be empowered to recognize narcissistic patterns and protect yourself if you find yourself in a similar situation.

Journaling to a
Positive Mindset

The combination of journaling and gratitude is incredibly powerful. The following journal excerpts came directly from Maria's journal during a four-month period in 2011. You will witness here what can happen in a short period when, with intention, you decide to create a new experience for yourself.

August 14, 2011

He called me and said, "Maria, I couldn't wait to get the fuck away from you!"

August 16, 2011

He asked to have breakfast with me. He confessed to cheating and having sex with the girl that I knew he was cheating with. I asked him if he had feelings for her.

He said: "I don't know, I am confused."

I told him I had filed for divorce and that he would probably get the papers today. He said he didn't want divorce, he wanted to work things out, that he loved me very much. He pretended to cry. Said he wanted to kiss me but was afraid he wouldn't be able to let go. He asked me on a date for Friday.

August 17, 2011

He texted me saying the date was off. Said he could not sit for two hours looking at me.

August 18, 2011

He sends me an e-mail saying he wants a divorce. Refused to talk to me on the phone or face to face. I went to his work and waited outside for 30 minutes because I knew he was done with work. He knew I was waiting for him but was a pussy and didn't come out, so I went home.

August 19, 2011

He was served divorce papers at around noon, and he refused them.

August 20, 2011

Kids spent the weekend at the grandparents. When they called me, they said:
"Mommy, Daddy has the computer right here, and it's connected with wires to the phone."
Benny was extremely quiet, and I asked him if he was okay and what was wrong. He said: "I don't know, mommy, I don't know what to say." I couldn't tell my kids I was being recorded and that my son understood what was happening.

August 23, 2011

He called me on the land line yelling at me. Was nasty and started acting very passive aggressive. Told me to stop saying that he abandoned me and the kids.

He started yelling and wouldn't let me get a word, then he hung up the phone.

About an hour later he sent me an email as if nothing had happened telling me he was going to be on the early show. He was acting as if nothing had happened before.

He called the landline, and my son was talking to him. My son put him on speakerphone because his friend was over. I could hear Darius say: "Benny, you break my heart when you say you don't want to talk to me because your friend is over. Whose is more important your friend or I? I went outside disgusted by what I was hearing, but when I came back inside he was saying: "Benny you know the water you take baths in? The lights at night, the house, the bills? I am paying for all that not mommy. Daddy isn't there but I am paying for everything. Mommy gets $275 a week and daddy gets $225."

I asked Benny if I could take his father off speakerphone to talk to him. Benny said "Yes."

So, I said to Darius: "What are you doing to these kids?!Why are you saying these things to a 7-year-old?! I am getting sick and tired of you telling our kids this. You are not paying for everything. You forget I used to make more money than you. I've worked harder than you and still was a full-time mom while you were messing around cheating. You left, not us!"

He started cutting me off and started talking over me: "I'm a good dad, Maria; I take them on the weekends and feed them!"

I said: "Darius I have them Monday through Friday. You left us Darius. You did this to us. I am the one who is ALWAYS, ALWAYS here for these kids. You are NEVER here for them, you put your little theatre gigs first always." He again, started cutting me off.

"Darius this is why- you keep saying you want us to be friends, but I can't even have a conversation with you without you arguing with me, you scream and get loud, this is why our attorneys are the ones that need to handle this."

He said, "Oh yeah, your attorney, he's a winner! He already screwed up and gave me bonus points."

Later that day, he sent me an email:

"Maria, I really don't want to fight with you."

I responded: "Darius, you love to fight. Go back to all the emails you've sent me since you abandoned your family. Your emails are simply drama, wanting to start fights and picking arguments. I am tired of drama and you treating me like GARBAGE. I don't deserve this!

You have no respect for me. I've been your wife all these years. I don't deserve how you have treated me. If you don't love me anymore, then you should have been man enough to tell me so. I am tired, Darius, of being your TOY and controlled by you. I have really been trying hard to be your friend after you broke my heart and all your lies, and still, you keep wanting to fight. You made the choice. This is what you wanted. Please be happy, Darius. I am not a piece of shit. Go look for whatever you are looking for. Please do not email me anymore unless it's about our children or be a man and talk to me face to face."

August 25, 2011

He came to the house. He was mean. I asked him for the password for my phone account so that I could see the bill because the phone wasn't working. He refused to give it to me and said: Technically it's not your phone. I signed up for it for you." I said: Darius, we are married. I wanted to get my own phone, but you insisted you get it through your work discount and had control over my phone all these years." I asked if he could please look into it and give me the password. He said, "No!"

Later in the day I tried calling the phone company and explained the situation. They said they could call him to ask for his permission to transfer the phone. He not only denied it, but he disconnected my service and canceled my number.

I sent him an email and expressed my concern because that was the only way I would be able to communicate with our children when he took them on the weekends. He sent me an email back:

How dare you question my decision to terminate the phone contract. You made that happen, Maria, not me!"

I went out and got another phone with the help of one of my students.

August 26, 2011

I have so many things to write about that I don't even know how and where to start. I'm sitting here in my kitchen listening to music. My husband abandoned me and my three children on July 28th, and ever since then, my life has been turned upside down. I'm also staring at an e-mail he sent to me today and I want to reply so bad but this time I'm not going to. I don't know what it was but something happened inside me last night that made me realize more than ever that something is wrong with my husband and now he's playing mind games with me. Even though I'm sitting here alone right now I don't feel alone or even scared anymore. I feel a strong force inside and all around me. It's so strong I can't even explain. I must have read my husband's e-mail about 6 times, and every time I finish, instead of crying like I have been up until now, I have to laugh and really feel bad for him. After everything he has done to me, he is still blaming me for all his lies and bad behavior it's so sad when people think their lies are true. That's so strong he says he's not happy I told him before no one can make him happy and it's no one's fault. You as a person have to be happy with your own self. I have faith in God.

August 28, 2011

That's exactly 1 month since my husband abandoned my children and I our two dogs and our everything. It's been a tough day on me because yesterday we spent the day together celebrating our daughter's birthday. Every time he emails, texts, he's being or talks to me, there's my balance off because he broke my heart and hasn't shown any remorse for what he did to our children or me. Up until now he has me all figured out, he knows how I'll react and how to push my button. I feel like we are in a cycle but this time I need to do something different. I need to become independent and stop melting for him. So that's exactly what I did at my daughter's party. If he wants to be divorced from me, has treated me like garbage and like I'm not even his wife then it's time for me to do the same. But I am still wearing my wedding ring. We were at the restaurant he sat next to me and as always, he was indecisive about what drink he would get he got coke but then he said it tasted like root beer so he sent it back then he said it tastes the same. He always does this. Can't make up his mind. While we were sitting there eating he says to me: "If you want to go out next week let me know what day and time." I said: "What do you mean? Go out go out for what? To talk about us or just to go out?" He replied "Oh, it doesn't matter". So, I said: "If it's to go out to talk about us, I'm not ready yet, but if it's just to go out, I'll think about it and let you know."

When we got to the car he said: "You and Charlena are the best dressed people in the entire place. Gave me a big hug lifted me from the ground had his hands on my waist and kissed my lips. The kids saw and started saying "Yay, Mommy and Daddy are kissing; they are together again they aren't fighting!"

He said to me that he had a lot of free time on Monday because he had to go to work at 3:30 AM and to let him know if I wanted to go out with him after. I told him I would let him know. I got in the car he went around my car and placed the kiss on my passenger side window, leaving his lip marks. Then he was pointing at it like a little kid. He confuses the fuck out of me. I don't know what to think.

A. he is either really confused and doesn't know what the fuck he wants and truly misses me.
B. he's playing with my feelings and is fucking with me because he knows he's going to get fucked and doesn't want us to have attorneys involved or
C. he doesn't love me and just wants us to be friends.

Something isn't right for sure. Maybe it's all of the above. Who knows.

August 29, 2011

I made a vision board with our pictures, and this time, underneath I wrote in big letters:

God, I want my husband back—fixed. Make him see the light and believe in you.

I had a rosary bead that I wanted to give him on Sunday, but I forgot it at home, so I plan on mailing it to him tomorrow. I wrote a note inside: let God guide you. Pray, Darius. God will show you the light.

I saw a marriage counselor, and he said there is no such thing as a midlife crisis and that it's just a term used to excuse bad behavior. He said my husband has been cheating on me and is projecting now. He asked me why would I want him back. But he did say that if I took him back that I should make him go through six months of therapy. I keep praying and talking to God keep my faith. However, today, I'm not sure if it's because I'm feeling sad; I don't feel the flow and positivity I felt yesterday. God help me through this. I want my husband and my family back. But I want my husband to come back fixed—a new man who will love me for who I am, appreciate everything I do, treat me with respect and put me above everything else. Treat me as his wife not a toy.

August 30, 2011

What a fucking day from hell, thanks to my asshole husband. He really pissed me off today, all day. I texted him to give him my new number so he could contact me if he needed to reach kids. He started giving me a hard time about me getting a new phone. If he hadn't cancelled my phone, I wouldn't have had to get a new one. It's his fault, his doing.

August 31, 2011

I feel good when I don't hear from Darius. He pulls my energy and drains me with his drama. I've started studying the law of attraction. It's complicated, but it makes sense.

A. Want something?
B. Define what you want

C. Get a hold of the feeling
D. Watch it unfold

Monday, September 5, 2011

My friend Janneth told me to write a list of blessings/a gratitude journal and meditate twice daily. Give love to people as much as you can. Don't talk about things you don't want.

Thank you God for my children.

Thank you God for me being able to talk to my husband today without us fighting.

Thank you, God, that he said he misses talking to me and hugging me.

Thank you, God, that my husband texted me saying he misses everyone.

Thank you, God, for my friend Janet. I love her.

Thank you, God, for my home.

Thank you, God, for my car.

Thank you, God, for my doggies.

Thank you, God, for my smile.

Thank you, God, for my body.

Thank you, God, for my fish.

Thank you, God, for my family, aunt, and cousins.

Thank you, God, for having my grandfather looking over me.

I love you, God!

You are AWESOME, God, and I love you and all things you have created.

Amen.

My friend sent me a YouTube video on how to meditate. I just finished doing that, and it felt so good. It was a deep experience. My mind wandered off for a few seconds, but I immediately brought myself back, and at that moment, I felt that I was more than just a human being, more than just a body, a physical thing—I was a spirit, there is a strong force inside me, and it's amazing. I want to share this with everyone. We can control our path and who we are—it's amazing. Life is a game. You just need to learn to play it right, and to do that, you must believe you must be aligned with your true self.

I love it!

It's hard work, but it's real, and I think once I'm there aligned, it won't be hard at all to stay there because it will always feel good. Being in the flow. I used to hear all the time people say

"Life is a secret."

This is the secret; you just need to find that force of God within us. We are all the same. Wow! Amazing stuff.

September 6, 2011

I ended last night writing about the law of attraction. This vortex stuff is amazing, and now I'm starting my day by saying and feeling the same thing. Still in flow. Until my ex called a little over 8 AM. He brought my flow and energy down, but right after he hung up, I started watching videos from Ester and Jerry about being in the vortex and being able to align yourself.

God, thank you for the great time I had at the movies last night.

God, thank you for the walk this morning.

God, thank you for Robin, Sarah, and Jake. Thank you for all the friends I made today.

God, thank you for my babies.

God, thank you for the meal that my friends made today.

God, thank you for everything, from my house, my dogs, my car, and my life.

I love you, God, thank you.

September 11, 2011

God, thank you for my neighbors.
God, thank you for today.
God, thank you for my children.
God, thank you for the great time that I've had with them.
God, thank you for me.
God, thank you for my house.
God, thank you for my car.
God, thank you for Abraham's videos.
Thank you, God, I love you.

September 17, 2011

You learn so much about yourself when you go through a divorce. I am discovering a new Maria. My friend laughs at me and says I had an epiphany because up until last Thursday, I kept saying I wanted my husband back even after everything that he's done to me, how he's treated me, and the mean things he said.

I know in my heart that what we had for the past ten years was real and that the man that I married is buried and trapped in that body, but he's lost and doesn't know how to get out.

Anyway... it wasn't until I went to a counselor last Thursday that I woke up. What he said made so much sense. He's so good; this was my third time going to see him. He said I'm an artist and that Darius has been my project all these years. My job has been to polish him and make him feel secure in himself. When I finally started to think about myself, that's when my marriage started falling apart because he started to realize he can no longer control me. He didn't like the fact that I was getting more attention than him. He's a narcissist, and he's been projecting on me. He doesn't have the guts or courage to see himself for who he is, so it's easier for him to take it out on me. The counselor also said we need to find out why he has so much control over me and why I feel intimidated by him. He says he's going to help me figure out when that happened and why.

I also told him that when Darius emails or texts, I feel claustrophobic. I can be fine for days, but as soon as he sends me an e-mail or text, I start to feel claustrophobic because he sucks all my positive energy.

That's also when I realized Darius used to say to me all the time, "You are my fountain of youth!" He was so right in that. I am his fountain of youth. Since he's been married to me, he looks like he's 20 years younger than what he used to look like. I made him who he is today. I polished him, but I wasted 10 years of my life in his shadow when I should have been the one out there. But you know what? I have no regrets. It's never too late. My time is now. God does everything right, and everything happens for a reason.

Right now, I'm sitting outside selling stuff at my garage sale. Darius has the kids, and he's throwing a party for my baby's 5th birthday. I didn't tell him I was selling stuff. Whatever. He wants me to pay the bills, I'll pay the bills with the money I make today. It's so painful putting stuff out to sell because it's part of us. But there is no more us. I think the part that hurts the most is the fact that he's not even sorry about anything that he has done. It's like he has no feelings, no emotions and is taking everything as a big joke. He's acting like a teenager, like a child. My family has been so supportive. They were the main foundation that helped me get through this entire situation.

The first 3 weeks were so painful and hard to handle. You really need family and a great support group to get through something so painful as what I am going through. At first, I didn't know what was going on. I guess I was in shock. Things were great between us. We had just gone to a beautiful vacation and a baseball game as a family and had such a good time.

The day he left, he said he didn't want to leave the house to go after booty. He said: "Maria, I know you don't believe me when I say I want to take you out on dates, but you'll see. You think I just want to go out and have sex or be with other women. You'll see Maria. You are hot, gorgeous, smart, talented. Why would I want other women? I just need to find myself and fix everything. We have 3 beautiful children, and I love you very much." He lied about everything. He made things worse. My brother says he told me what I wanted to hear, and it's so true. He was playing with my feelings and my emotions.

God, thank you for being you.

God, thank you for not leaving me alone.

God, thank you for hearing my prayers.

God, thank you for guiding me Through this rough time.

God, thank you for my brother.

God, thank you for my children.

God, thank you for my parents.

God, thank you for my house, my car, and my dogs.

I love you, God.

October 11, 2011

I'm in LA today at church, waiting for mass to start.

One of my girlfriends bought me this flight to get me away from Darius on my birthday.

She is singing in mass today.

God, thank you! I feel your presence more than ever. This is an amazing experience I'm going through. I want to tell the entire world about you. You are in me; I am yours, God, to do whatever you want.

Thank you for giving me this beautiful gift. I love you, God.

Please help my friend achieve her goal of becoming a singer. She is also a believer in you, God.

Want something?

Define what you want!

Get a hold of that feeling.

Watch it Unfold.

November 21, 2011

This is so weird. It's been quite some time since I wrote this diary. So many things have happened since my last entry. I was just reading what I wrote and it's amazing how the law of attraction works. In August, I wrote that I wanted my husband to come back. I defined what I wanted, held on to that feeling, and watched it unfold. It happened. I wrote down that he was coming home before the holidays. Everyone thought I was crazy and kept saying he was not coming back. He did. But the only problem was I ripped the word "fix" out of the sentence. I had a big strip along my vision board in my bedroom that said: "God, please bring my husband back fixed." After studying the law of attraction and listening to some Abraham videos, I realized you can't ask the universe to change someone. So, I ripped the word "fixed" out.

Darius got on his knees begging me not to divorce him and to take him back. He looked like a desperate psychopath. At that moment, I heard a voice saying, "You are going to be okay." I told him to get up. I told him it was over.

He wants to come back, but he has no remorse for what he's done to me or our family. So much has happened. I don't even know where to start. I just know I need to break this cycle once and for all. I need to focus on my dream. So, I'm going to try this again. I know what I want and I'm going to define it. I'm going to get a hold of the feeling, and I have one month to watch it unfold. My last wish on my vision board took about a little over one month to unfold. Let's see how long this one will take: "I want to launch my own company and host my own online show."

My intention has been set. Now, I'm going to hang on to the feeling and watch it unfold. I know it's going to happen. The power of manifestation.

December 6, 2011

Life is amazing, and it's so amazing that it's illegal. So many things have happened in my life in the past four months, so many changes, so many obstacles, even last week. So many things happened last week, and here I am now saying life is amazing while I only have $100 to my name right now (LMAO)

God has shown me that money isn't everything! God will always provide what you need if you have faith and belief. I believe in God more than ever. God is amazing, I'm amazing. I'm God, and God is in me. In Philippians 4: 6-7, it says: "Be anxious for nothing. But in anything by prayer and supplication with thanksgiving let your requests be made known to God and the power of God which surpasses all understanding will guard your hearts and minds through Christ Jesus."

God, thank you so much for this wonderful day!
I forgive Darius.
God forgive me for my sins. I know I'm a Sinner. We are all sinners.
I love you with all my heart!

I believe in you more than ever.

Thank you for my children. They are angels.

Thank you for my doggie, Pantufa.

Thank you for my house.

Thank you for my car.

Thank you for all the contacts I made today and the contract I signed with WNFOX.

Thank you for the calls that I received from Senator Young's office offering me a job

Thank you for the call that I received from the radio station offering me a job

Thank you for the e-mail that I received from the newspaper offering me a job

Thank you, God, for my body, my temple.

Thank you, God, for being you, and I love you, God, and believe in you. I surrender and want to be at peace.

December 10, 2011

I have had an amazing experience in my life over the past four months. I thought I lost everything, but I only gained. I gained God, and I am awake. I am not afraid, and I know that I am never alone. God listens to me and everyone who talks to me and follows his word.

Thank you, God, for the $3,000 check

Thank you, God, for allowing me to pay back my neighbor the money I borrowed from her for the private investigator

Thank you, God, for the doll house that I was able to buy for my daughter.

Thank you, God, for this weekend's fashion show at the fundraiser and all the nice comments from everyone.

Thank you, God, for the check from the TV station.

Thank you, God, for my children.

Thank you, God, for Darius. I've learned so much.

Thank you, God, for teaching me to love myself and be confident about myself.

Thank you, God, for taking care of me and not letting me sink.

Thank you, God, for loving me.

Thank you, God, for everything that I have.

Thank you, thank you, thank you.

I love you, God. I love you!

Faith wins over fear always!

December 13, 2011

Thank you, Lord, for such a wonderful day. This was a beautiful day from beginning to end.

You are amazing. Thank you for being with me all the way. I love myself so much lately, and it's all thanks to you, my Lord.

Thank you for all my show sponsors.

Thank you, God, for my beautiful children. They are the love of my life, and I adore them.

Thank you, God, for never leaving me. I feel amazing again and sexy, very confident about myself thanks to you, my Lord.

December 16, 2011

It's 1:00 AM, and I'm exporting video promos to social media. I want to take this moment and thank you, God, for everything in my life. Thank you for my children.

Thank you for my house.

Thank you for my doggie, Pantufa.

Thank you for my car.

Thank you for my body.

Thank you for giving me an amazing life.

Thank you for protecting me from having an accident today when that guy almost hit me and ran me off the road.

Thank you for protecting me.

I love you, Lord, and I am forever grateful for everything you do and put in my life. I know I'm not alone.

I hear your voice, my Lord.

Guide me and take all my worries. I want to be in peace and awake so I can hear you every day, every minute.

Please, God, give me the push that I need to launch my business.

December 20, 2011

This was an amazing day, Lord. God, you gave me more money.

You work in mysterious ways, and I love it. I had no idea I had this much money in my account.

Thank you.

It felt so good when I was at the bank and got that money out.

Thank you, God, for giving me the money so that I could buy the laptop for my son for Christmas.

Thank you for the doll house and thank you for the kitchen for my kiddos.

God, I know you're taking care of me and are looking out for me.

When I'm with you, I feel so at peace. I love you, and you are teaching me so much.

Keep taking all my worries and troubles.

I know you have a plan for me, and I want to serve you, Lord.

I don't want to fail.

Author's Note

Maria's story reflects not only her desires but also the immense power of intention and positivity.

As she learned more about resiliency in difficult situations and creating a life she loves, she set her intentions to paper and began taking steps to bring her desired life into reality. As a way of solidifying her belief that everything she wants is possible, she asked me to include a written vision of a life she wanted, defined, got hold of the feeling, and saw it all unfold.

Go, Maria! We are cheering you on.

I, Maria Crowe, found the love of my life, a man who cherishes me not only for my outer beauty but also for my heart and my mind. Together, we are traveling the world in pure harmony, our bond deepening each day into a profound friendship, romance, and mutual care.

We are creating unforgettable memories as we become bound by authentic love. He is my best friend, passionate lover, and unwavering partner.

Our relationship is filled with abundant wealth, vibrant health, and endless joy as we build a life of peace, happiness, and deep connection. We wake up each day to enjoy coffee together as the sun rises and end the day falling asleep in each other's arms. Our hearts are full. He looks at me adoringly and tells me how much he loves me.

He proposed to me in the most magical way.

My children are thriving on their paths as successful individuals who hold a special love for God in their hearts.

My son has become a renowned game developer and now owns his own gaming company. My daughters became successful medical doctors. I am so proud that they treat their patients and staff with kindness and compassion, and they are loving individuals who create beautiful, happy lives for themselves and others.

My story is reaching millions of people, inspiring them to become more resilient through the power of positivity. Through my work and inner strength, I have become extremely wealthy in my own right, helping countless individuals and families worldwide.

You, too, have the power to re-write your own story.

~Maria Crowe

Author Bio

Paula Fidalgo, an award-winning journalist, is renowned for her dedication to breaking news, earning an Associated Press award for her outstanding contributions in journalism. With a vast reporting experience spanning the capital region, CT, and MA, Paula's journalistic prowess has left an indelible mark on the field.

In 2015, Paula was honored with a nomination as one of Saratoga County's most influential women, a testament to her impactful presence in the community. Her commitment to social causes was further highlighted when she was crowned National Miss in 2016, championing the cause of breaking the silence surrounding domestic violence. Paula's exemplary service has been recognized on numerous occasions, including being awarded two bronze medal awards by President Obama in 2015 and 2016, as well as being commended by Governor Cuomo for her outstanding volunteerism efforts in 2016.

With a passion for education, Paula served as the Director of Education for the New School of Radio and Television, empowering aspiring professionals in the media industry. Additionally, she has been a driving force as a committee member for BPW (Business Professional Women) of Schenectady, where she actively participates in fundraising initiatives to support young women in their pursuit of higher education through scholarships. Paula's dedication to community outreach extends to her advocacy for domestic violence awareness and support, notably in her role as a supporter of the Domestic Violence in Mechanicville.

As President of the BNI Business Exchange Leaders Clifton Park chapter, she fosters a culture of collaboration and growth among local business leaders. Beyond her professional endeavors, Paula's philanthropic spirit shines through her initiatives such as "TeddyBear Hugs," where she collected teddy bears for nursing homes, spreading kindness and joy to those in need. As the Founder, CEO, and President of The Dust Busters and Fidalgo Enterprises, local cleaning companies, Paula demonstrates her entrepreneurial acumen and commitment to community service.

Paula is a proud 46er, having conquered all 46 High Peaks in New York State over the course of four summers. These rugged hikes tested both physical endurance and mental strength, providing her with a powerful form of mind training. Each ascent was a lesson in perseverance, resilience, and the rewards of pushing past limits. Though grueling at times, reaching each summit brought an unmatched sense of accomplishment and connection to nature.

Paula also had a brush with Hollywood, appearing as an extra in Steven Spielberg's 2005 blockbuster War of the Worlds, starring Tom Cruise. Filmed in part in Athens, New York, the experience gave her a fascinating behind-the-scenes look at the world of filmmaking. Being on set, witnessing the creative process, and seeing a major production come to life remains a memorable and unique chapter in her journey.

Furthermore, Paula holds certifications in Positive Psychology as both a practitioner and consultant, reflecting her dedication to holistic well-being and personal development.

Paula Fidalgo's remarkable journey exemplifies her unwavering commitment to journalism, advocacy, entrepreneurship, and community service, making her an inspirational figure in both professional and philanthropic circles.

You can learn more about Paula Fidalgo at www.paulafidalgo.com.